TARNISHED

# Tarnished

*Toxic Leadership in the
U.S. Military*

GEORGE E. REED

POTOMAC BOOKS
*An imprint of the University of Nebraska Press*

"The Contract: A Word from the Led,"
from *E-Mail from the Soul* by William
Ayot. Published by PS Avalon,
Glastonbury, UK, 2012. Reproduced by
permission of William Ayot.

Library of Congress Cataloging-in-
Publication Data
Reed, George E., 1958–
Tarnished: toxic leadership in the
U.S. military / George E. Reed.
pages   cm
Includes bibliographical references
and index.
ISBN 978-1-61234-723-3 (hardback: alk. paper)
ISBN 978-1-61234-801-8 (epub)
ISBN 978-1-61234-802-5 (mobi)
ISBN 978-1-61234-803-2 (pdf)
1. Command of troops.
2. United States—Armed Forces.
I. Title.
UB210.R395 2015
355.3'30410973—dc23
2015008305

Set in Minion by Westchester Publishing Services.

# CONTENTS

# PREFACE

Over twenty-five years ago, Joseph C. Rost, a professor at the University of San Diego, was struggling to better understand leadership. He was at the center of an experiment—an interdisciplinary program that had leadership as its central focus but not as a subset of management as in business administration, or imbedded in an institutional approach as in political science, or even as a product of personality or group dynamics as in psychology and sociology. James MacGregor Burns had already published his book *Leadership*, which forever changed how we look at leadership by expanding our view beyond traits, characteristics, and behaviors of leaders alone to include the important role of followers.[1] Burns took an interdisciplinary path with his career as well, starting out as a historian then directing his facile mind to political science and psychology. Burns was already well known for his biography of Franklin Delano Roosevelt *The Lion and the Fox* but before that he had served as a combat historian in the Pacific theater during World War II.[2] Rost had read voraciously—not everything that was written about leadership at the time, but a great deal of it. The remnants of his extensive leadership library can still be found at the University of San Diego's Department of Leadership Studies in the School of Leadership and Education Sciences.

Rost was underwhelmed by the treatment of the subject by most scholars and dismayed to find that most of the writers of the day never defined the subject they were writing about. For some leadership was a position, a predominate view that is mirrored in military organizations to this day. Other authors described leadership as a role or as good management. A few specified leadership as a process. Most did not take a stand one way or the other, leaving the reader to figure out what they were talking about. In his classic book *Leadership for the Twenty-First Century*, Rost crafted a carefully worded definition: "Leadership is an influence relationship among leaders and followers who intend real changes that reflect their mutual purposes."[3] He saw leadership as a multidirectional, noncoercive phenomenon that requires two or more people who are purposeful in their in relationship. Both leader and follower are motivated by a common purpose to achieve substantive and transforming change. Rost asserted that leadership exists outside of formal roles and authoritative positions.

This book continues in the tradition of those who see followers as an important and sometimes overlooked element in the leadership dynamic. I did not write this book because I was abused as a lieutenant. All lieutenants were abused at some point or another, and we took it all in stride as the way things were. I experienced far more exemplary leadership than bad over my twenty-seven years in the army. Perhaps that is why the few bad ones stand out so vividly in my memory. What struck me even at an early stage of development was a nagging question: Why would an organization so obviously focused on good leadership put up with and in some cases facilitate bad leaders? In leadership doctrine all the examples were positive and aspirational, yet that is not what many in uniform experienced.

I care deeply about all branches of the armed forces and have an abiding affection for my brothers and sisters in uniform. If anything in these pages comes off as excessively critical, it is my hope that it will be accepted as a friendly critique by one who sincerely cares about the profession of arms. Underneath the growth of facial hair and extra pounds added since retirement beats the heart of a soldier.

*Tarnished: Toxic Leadership in the U.S. Military* is an attempt to understand destructive leadership better. This undertaking follows four journal articles on the topic and countless presentations. It is meant to be scholarly, yet accessible to a broad audience interested in military leadership and especially those who are currently serving in uniform. As a result I have portrayed research findings without the annotating $P$ values, sample sizes, and statistical tables. Those are available in the original research works that are cited throughout. Chapter 1 introduces the subject and explores a number of definitions while suggesting that in a democratic society it is important to be concerned about leadership style. Chapter 2 addresses the "so what?" question by examining the impact of toxic leadership as evidenced by extant leadership with a specific focus on studies using military samples. Chapter 3 examines how system dynamics in military organizations can create or perpetuate toxic leadership. Chapter 4 takes a look at the role of narcissism in toxic leadership, a related construct that explains the source of some destructive behaviors. Chapter 5 addresses an issue of contemporary interest: sexual misconduct that falls within the definition of toxic behavior. Chapter 6 was written to provide insight for those who find themselves in the unenviable position of working for a toxic leader. Chapter 7 is a brief exploration of toxic coworkers and what can be done about them. Chapter 8 identifies steps that military organizations can consider as they try to minimize toxic leadership, with a focus on ways to identify and deal with destructive leadership through organizational systems and processes. The conclusion touches on some of the ethical considerations of toxic leadership before summarizing key arguments.

*George E. Reed*
*San Diego CA*

# ACKNOWLEDGMENTS

I am grateful for the support of the University of San Diego, which provided the encouragement to write this book as well as access to brilliant students such as James Dobbs and Melanie Hitchcock who helped shape my thinking on the topic. I am equally grateful to my faculty colleagues in the Department of Leadership Studies, who in addition to being a fine group of scholars also happen to be genuinely good people. I have benefitted much from their support and good counsel. I am thankful for and humbled by the many who have called or written to tell me of their trials and tribulations at the hands of toxic leaders. I would be most pleased if they saw some purpose in their suffering through this publication. I also thank my valued colleague R. Craig Bullis from the U.S. Army War College, who was there at the beginning of this journey, and Rick Olsen, who provided access to students at Fort Leavenworth as well as able collaboration. I am especially indebted to Lieutenant General Walter F. Ulmer Jr., USA Ret., for his unflagging support and mentorship. I am also grateful for the encouragement of Alicia Christensen of Potomac Books who convinced me the time was right for this book.

A salute is appropriate to my former commanders and supervisors who patiently tolerated my many missteps along the way and to the soldiers who served so ably and loyally with me. To my former company commander Ken Allen, I am sorry for the many dressings-down you suffered for my boneheaded stunts. I'm so pleased we can laugh about it now. To the two finest supervisors I have ever had, Brigadier Generals (Ret.) Daniel Doherty and David Foley, I give heartfelt thanks for the many examples of outstanding leadership you provided. I hope to see you all on the high ground someday.

I apologize to my saintly wife, Lucy, for my absence and inconsiderate single-minded focus on the writing of this book to the exclusion of all other things. My only excuse is that I was defenseless against the pull of the work.

I dedicate this book to my late father, Private Bennie F. Reed, USMC, a stoic member of the greatest generation. He was a quiet, hardworking, and dignified man who taught so much to his son, and always by example.

# 1   Nature and Scope of Toxic Leadership

> The discipline which makes the soldiers of a free country reliable in battle is not to be gained by harsh or tyrannical treatment. On the contrary, such treatment is far more likely to destroy than to make an army. It is possible to impart instructions and to give commands in such a manner and in such a tone of voice as to inspire in the soldier no feeling but an intense desire to obey, while the opposite manner and tone of voice cannot fail to excite strong resentment and a desire to disobey. The one mode or other of dealing with subordinates springs from a corresponding spirit in the breast of the commander. He who feels the respect which is due others cannot fail to inspire in them regard for himself; while he who feels, and hence manifests, disrespect toward others, especially his inferiors, cannot fail to inspire hatred against himself.
> —Major General John M. Schofield, 1879

Leadership is a favored and important construct of the U.S. military. Its service academies are charged to produce responsible leaders of character, an extensive and expensive system of professional military education schools and courses endeavors to enhance leadership skills at all levels, and those in positions of authority are vested with extraordinary levels of power and responsibility. Each service publishes copious amounts of leadership doctrine and guidance materials that seek to inculcate a common view of what is expected of those in positions of authority. Leadership is viewed not only as a role or process but also as a solution to almost any problem. Public debacles, scandals, or failings are frequently explained, in part, as a failure of leadership. Leaders, especially those in positions of command, are deemed accountable for everything their unit does or fails to do; as a result, when military organizations perform poorly, leaders are frequently replaced. It is an approach that has generally served the nation well in light of the unique context in which the military operates.

The military context is different from many others, distinctive and unique for its association with the employment of violence on behalf of the state. Democracies have an ambiguous relationship with their militaries. The state depends on its standing military to safeguard it, but the military also represents a potential threat to democracy—thus the concerns expressed by our founding fathers and their preference for defense based on militias raised from the citizenry in times of crisis. Such concerns also serve to explain why leadership is a central construct in the military. Formations that are well led and controlled by those who have a nuanced understanding of the role of the military in a democratic society serve as a protection of the republic. It is no wonder that military leadership tends to be more structured and professionalized than in other sectors of society. Discipline, clear lines of authority manifested in a command, and a control-oriented focus are not simply vestiges of bureaucracy; they are also a means to contain an organization that has access to a great deal of destructive power.

The military also requires an exceptional level of commitment from its members. Military service is synonymous with sacrifice, involving long periods of separation from family members, frequent moves and deployments, the rigors of intensive training, and the horrors of combat. A military life is rewarding, but it is also hard, exacting a toll that is both physical and emotional. The environment is frequently dangerous, whether from attack by enemies of the state or in the performance of high-risk operations using weapons and heavy equipment. The air and sea are inherently unforgiving environments even without an enemy to fight. The modern U.S. military is an all-recruited force that depends on attracting and retaining enough qualified men and women who are willing to serve despite the associated dangers and rigors. It is drawn mostly from an increasingly small subsection of the larger citizenry, a fit and youthful population mostly between eighteen and twenty-five years of age. It is both an enthusiastic and occasionally unruly demographic.

When it comes to organizational outcomes, the stakes are high in military organizations. The penalty for poor performance extends beyond profit and loss to include the lives of both military personnel and noncombatants. Those in positions of authority in military organizations are constantly reminded of the costs associated with insufficient training, inadequate equipment, and poor strategy. Because the military serves as the guarantor of security for the nation, the cost of military failure can be catastrophic for a society. The public rightly expects a high level of performance and disciplined execution of duties. Personal failures and flaws tolerated by leaders in other sectors are less likely to be forgiven in the military. Americans seem to equally relish putting their leaders on pedestals and knocking them off: Americans may well be prone to a form of hero worship where military leaders are respected and exalted, but the public is also unforgiving when it perceives its trust and confidence were misplaced.

The American people have a relatively high level of confidence in the leadership of their military. The Harvard Kennedy School Center for Public Leadership publishes an annual National Leadership Index that surveys public confidence in the leadership of thirteen sectors.[1] The military is, and has been, the institution in American society that rates the highest level of leadership confidence. On a scale of confidence ranging from "none at all" to "a great deal," the military is the only sector that reached the great deal of confidence level.[2] It is remarkable that the military holds such a position of confidence after over a decade of protracted conflict, with the inevitable mistakes and public missteps associated with combat operations. In the court of public opinion, the stories of bravery and sacrifice compete with those of senior officer misconduct and atrocities. When the military performs its duties well and meets the expectations of the broader society, it builds confidence and goodwill. When it fails to meet those expectations, confidence is diminished. Still, in terms of leadership, the military is clearly doing something right in the eyes of the public, though we might question whether such a high opinion is based on full knowledge as the professionalized army is increasingly distant from the populace it serves.

The relative lack of understanding most Americans have about their military is a double-edged sword. On the one hand, the distance between the average citizen and the military is a sign of success. The more a professionalized military does its job well, the less attention the average civilian must devote to issues of national defense. That leaves military professionals to apply their craft without excessive interference or meddling. To some degree, ignorance of the military is also evidence of trust and confidence. On the other hand, such benign neglect does not serve the nation or its military well. Uneducated overconfidence can result in the unwise application of military power, and unfettered admiration can lead to unquestioning and excessive deference with regard to military matters. Excessive deference can be problematic when bad, destructive, abusive, or toxic leadership practices that would not be acceptable in other sectors are allowed to go unchecked in the armed services.

There are legitimate reasons why military practices occasionally vary from those in the larger society. Prosecuting military offenses such as desertion and failure to obey a lawful order are necessary to instill discipline. The military justice system is designed to enable the application of law in an expeditionary force in foreign lands where access to the civilian court system is inconvenient if not impossible. Yet such exceptions should be carefully considered and justified, not granted as a blank check out of ignorance and inattention. An article in the *Atlantic* decried the lack of effective congressional oversight:

> Politicians say that national security is their first and most sacred duty, but they do not act as if this is so. The most recent defense budget passed the House Armed Services Committee by a vote of 61 to zero, with similarly one-sided debate before the vote. This is the same House of Representatives that cannot pass a long-term Highway Trust Fund bill that both parties support. "The lionization of military officials by politicians is remarkable and dangerous," a retired Air Force colonel named Tom Ruby, who now writes on organizational culture, told me. He and others said that this deference was one reason so little serious oversight of the military took place.[3]

There is an unstated contract with American families in terms of expectations regarding leadership. The flower of American youth is the raw material the military requires to operate. Mothers and fathers send their sons and daughters to the armed services, probably with some reservations but mostly with consent, with the understanding that their children will be given opportunities to learn and develop under the tutelage of good leaders. Through the intensive socialization process of basic and advanced training, young men and women become soldiers, sailors, airmen, and marines. When their service is complete, they tell friends and family about their experiences, thereby influencing others to enlist as well. It is understood that the military environment is dangerous and that safety cannot be guaranteed, but it is also anticipated that loved ones will be cared for as best as practicable and treated with respect. Unfortunately, the terms of this contract are not always met.

## Describing Toxic Leadership

Leadership can be viewed on a spectrum, with exemplary, motivating, and inspiring behavior on one end and demotivating, belittling, and disrespectful behavior at the other. All those who attempt to lead can be placed somewhere along that spectrum. Some in positions of authority add value to their organizations through a leadership style that raises morale, energizing and uplifting the organizational climate in the process. Others demoralize subordinates through a self-serving, inflexible, and petty style that has a negative impact on the organizational climate.

There are two things to keep in mind when talking about leadership style. First, leadership style is a pattern of behavior over time as perceived by the targets of influence. That is, the intentions of a leader are less important than the perceptions of the followers. It is not a single behavior or instance that marks a problematic or destructive leadership style—every supervisor has a bad day once in a while. Rather, it is a pattern of behavior and the impact over time that tell the tale. Second, style has little to do with competence or dedication. Some who appear to be devoid of interpersonal skills can manifest brilliance and be highly competent in the technical or cognitive domain. Stonewall Jackson, for example, was one of the most venerated confederate generals of the American Civil War. As a battlefield commander, he was appreciated for his tactical proficiency and dependability. Before the Civil War, however, his dour nature and peculiar habits had earned him the nickname "Tom Fool Jackson" among students at the Virginia Military Academy. As a brevet major assigned to Fort Meade, he was subject to a brooding anger, as demonstrated in his squabble with a fellow officer that earned him a stern reprimand from General Winfield Scott.[4] Jackson was quirky, but he was also an extremely effective leader in the crucible of war.

Those who attempt to lead with a destructive style are often highly dedicated and highly motivated to achieve the goals and objectives of the organization, but they go about accomplishing them in a manner that is counterproductive in the long run. When it comes to style, military leadership doctrine has been largely silent on this subject. That is probably appropriate because there is no one right way to influence others. No two leaders are exactly alike. What comes naturally to one person is awkward and inauthentic for another. Leaders are expected to harness their strengths and militate against their weaknesses. Some are naturally more affable or charismatic than others, but there are plenty of effective leaders who are introverted and more reserved in their interactions.

Proponents of situational leadership suggest that the best leadership style is the one that meets the needs of subordinates and the demands of a particular situation.[5] It is the responsibility of leaders to vary their approach based on what subordinates need and what a situation demands at a given point in time. There is a time to be loud and a time to be soft-spoken, a time to demand and a time to encourage or nurture. If the building is on fire, loud and emphatic direction is appreciated while that same behavior would be inappropriate in a different setting. If the enemy is inside the wire and the last rounds of ammunition are being counted, it is not the time to call for a focus group.

The most effective leaders seem to have an ability to identify the kind of intervention that is most likely to have a positive result, and they modify their behavior accordingly. As a result, we see a wide variation of leadership styles in practice as well as tolerance for a broad range of influence-behaviors. The range of tolerance for leadership style is sometimes too broad at the organizational level, permitting some who have an inappropriate style to have access to positions of authority and to remain in them too long. Supervisor-centric evaluations do not always discern between those who have a positive style and those who have a destructive impact. "Talented people in the 21st century expect to work in healthy climates, where strong bonds of mutual trust facilitate mission accomplishment and support long-term institutional strength,"[6] asserted W. F. Ulmer Jr. in a 2013 article on toxic leadership. Military personnel set a high bar for their superiors; inculcated along with respect for their superiors is the expectation that they will be led well.

In 2003 then secretary of the army Thomas E. White asked the U.S. Army War College to take a look at how the army might identify leaders who have a destructive leadership style. The result was a qualitative research study that used a series of focus groups to derive insights into the problem. That led to a report to the secretary of the army[7] and a *Military Review* article published in 2004.[8] Both publications are publicly available, but the backstory that prompted them is less widely known. Retired lieutenant general Walter F. Ulmer Jr. knew Secretary White from their mutual service in Germany during the Cold War. Ulmer, retired from a distinguished career that had included command of III Corps at Fort Hood, Texas, honed his academic interest in the study of leadership as the chief executive officer of the Center for Creative Leadership, a nonprofit organization that maintains one of the largest repositories of data on executives. For several years Ulmer informally canvassed a group of army colonels and lieutenant colonels for their experiences at the hands of senior leaders. What he found troubled him. Although his data collection methods and particularly his sampling process would not stand the scrutiny of the behavioral sciences, his convenience sample indicated that about 13 percent viewed their leaders as an obstruction to mission accomplishment, with leadership styles that were destructive to the long-term health and welfare of their units. Ulmer obtained an audience with the secretary of the army and asked him whether such numbers struck the secretary as satisfactory or an issue of concern. It was that question that prompted a question that had not been previously asked: What are we doing to identify and assess those who have a destructive leadership style? It was a very good question.

The armed services have long been successful in espousing the positive aspects of leadership. Military publications have typically focused more on the aspirations of good leadership than the lived experience in the field. Military doctrine on leadership is quite good at describing desired leadership behavior. It provides a common view of what leaders are expected to do at various levels of the organization. Leadership guru Peter Drucker reportedly once described the army's field manual on leadership (FM 22-100) as the single best document written on the subject. Meindl, Ehrlich, and Dukerich described an unrelenting positive social construction and commitment as the romance of leadership, but they saw the elevation of leadership to prominent and near mystical levels as exceeding the limits of what was substantiated by scientific inquiry.[9] The romance of leadership is perpetuated by a one-sided view of leadership bolstered by accounts of heroic leaders who are both inspiring and larger than life, distanced from our more mundane existence. Good leadership is indeed a wonderful thing, but what passes for leadership behavior in practice all too frequently falls short of aspirations.

Those who study leadership are aware of the problem of leadership attribution bias, a variant of the fundamental attribution error whereby observers tend to place unwarranted emphasis on individual characteristics to explain behavior rather than considering external factors. In other words, leaders are afforded more credit or blame than actually warranted for organizational success or failure. If an organization succeeds, leaders are credited; if an organization fails, leaders are blamed for it all, which underestimates the play of situational factors and chance. Although good leaders add value to organizations, some groups succeed despite miserable leadership, and others fail despite outstanding leadership. Good leadership is unlikely to resolve a fundamental resource–mission mismatch, just as good tactics are not likely to overcome a flawed strategy. Leadership, however, does make a difference, one that can be easily observed in military organizations where there are multiple wings, squadrons, companies, or batteries. They are manned, equipped, organized, and trained in nearly identical ways, yet an observer who spends a bit of time in each organization will identify visible differences in the attitudes of members and the feel of the units. Some of those differences are reflected in the attitudes and approaches of those in key positions of authority.

We do a disservice by depicting leadership in an exclusively positive light because "to deny bad leadership equivalence in the conversation is misguided, tantamount to a medical school that would claim to teach health while ignoring disease."[10] There is much to learn from negative examples; in fact, we may retain more from unpleasant or painful experiences than from those that were too easy. The impact of good events tends to dissipate more rapidly whereas bad events have longer lasting, more intense consequences.[11] Thus, bad leadership is not hard to recognize, especially when there are many examples of good leadership to compare it with.

There are many ways to lead badly. One classification scheme of bad leaders suggested descriptors such as incompetent, rigid, intemperate, callous, corrupt, insular, and evil. A classification scheme applied to the U.S. Army suggested another list of identifiable characteristics: incompetent, malfunctioning, maladjusted, inadequate, irresponsible, amoral, cowardly, insatiably ambitious, egotistic, arrogant, selfish, greedy, untrustworthy, deceptive, malicious, and malfeasant.[12] Although just about any negative adjective can be applied, such lists are helpful in painting a picture of what bad leadership looks like.

### Defining Toxic Leadership

Some definitional specificity is necessary to facilitate shared understanding and to prevent well-intentioned people from speaking past each other on the topic. There is no consensus definition among scholars who study toxic leadership, just as there is no universally accepted definition of leadership. It is an emerging term in an emerging field of study. Toxic leadership, the focus of this book, is closely related to other concepts such as abusive supervision, petty tyranny, workplace victimization, bullying, workplace psychopathy, brutal bosses, intolerable bosses, harassers, incivility, derailed leaders, and destructive leadership, so those interested in these phenomena should include such keywords in their search for references. The difficulty of defining toxic leadership is reminiscent of the task of defining obscenity, which once led Supreme Court Justice Potter Stewart to exclaim, "I know it when I see it."[13] In such cases it can be helpful to examine a series of proffered definitions, descriptions, and related concepts. They won't all align, but the process can result in a gestalt whereby the phenomenon can be recognized if not defined with great precision. Those who engage in research on the topic or who require a more structured definition can resort to explaining what they mean when using the term. There is a long history of using such operational definitions in the behavioral sciences.

A useful starting point for thinking about toxic leadership labels toxic leaders as those who "engage in numerous *destructive behaviors* and who exhibit certain *dysfunctional personal characteristics.* To count as toxic, these behaviors and qualities of character must inflict some reasonably serious and enduring harm on their followers and their organizations. The intent to harm others or enhance the self at the expense of others distinguishes seriously toxic leaders from the careless or unintentional toxic leaders, who also cause negative effects."[14] This definition identifies toxic leaders not only by their dysfunctional behavior but also by the extent of the harm they inflict on others and the organization. It also is helpful to consider a gradation of toxicity from careless and minor to intentional and seriously toxic. There may be many ways to be a bad leader, but the seriously toxic warrant a category of their own.

In *The Allure of Toxic Leaders*, Jean Lipman-Blumen did not engage in explaining the various levels of toxicity but instead focused on the role that followers play in facilitating such toxic leaders. She recognized that leadership requires two willing participants: leaders and followers. Leaders only have power when subordinates grant it to them. Most leadership scholars agree that leadership is best described as a voluntary relationship, distinguishing it from command or management, which involves compulsory compliance. Leadership is ratified in the hearts and minds of followers; if they don't consent to follow, leadership is not in effect.

Destructive leadership behavior can be defined as "the systematic and repeated behaviour by a leader, supervisor or manager that violates the legitimate interest of the organisation by undermining and/or sabotaging the organisation's goals, tasks, resources, and effectiveness and/or the motivation, well-being or job satisfaction of his/her subordinates."[15] The qualifiers of "systematic and repeated" contained in this definition exclude those who have had a one-off confrontation, and importantly there is a focus on the negative impact of destructive leadership on both the organization and its members. Note that intent is not part of this definition. Any behavior that has negative impact is included, even if it is unintentional. Destructive leaders may have the best of intentions and see their actions as fully justified, but they also cause harm in the process. Motivation, well-being, and job satisfaction are specifically highlighted as impact variables of interest.

Harvey Hornstein, professor emeritus of psychology and education at Columbia University, described "brutal bosses" without delineating a comprehensive definition, instead using words such as uncivil, cruel, humiliating, degrading, abusive, disrespectful, and hostile.[16] He sought to make a distinction between bosses who are tough and those who are abusive. Tough bosses set high standards and confront poor performance through a host of appropriate sanctions without stripping subordinates of their dignity. He proffered "eight deadly sins" that are characteristic of brutal bosses:

Deceit: Lying: giving false or misleading information through acts of omission or commission.
Constraint: Restricting subordinates' activities in domains outside of work, e.g., where they live, the people with whom they live, friendships, and civic activity.

Coercion: Threatening excessive or inappropriate harm for noncompliance with a boss's wishes.

Selfishness: Protecting themselves by blaming subordinates and making them scapegoats for any problems that occur.

Inequity: Providing unequal benefit or punishment to subordinates due to favoritism or non-work related criteria.

Cruelty: Harming subordinates in normally illegitimate ways, such as public humiliation, personal attack, or name-calling.

Disregard: Behaving in ways that violate ordinary standards of politeness and fairness, as well as displaying a flagrant lack of concern for subordinates' lives (e.g., "I don't give a damn about your family problems").

Deification: Implying a master-servant status in which bosses can do or say whatever they please to subordinates because they feel themselves to be superior people.[17]

Hornstein was less interested in organizational impact than in the presence of certain disrespectful behaviors that he deemed categorically wrong. Subordinates might ignore or manifest no negative impact from such abuse, but that does not excuse behavior that assaults the fundamental dignity of others.

Toxic leaders frequently engage in behavior that can be described as petty tyranny. Petty tyrants are those who lord their power over others in ways that are arbitrary, small-minded, oppressive, capricious, and vindictive.[18] One survey model to measure tyrannical behavior includes the following subcategories: being arbitrary and self-aggrandizing (using authority and position for personal gain, administering organizational policies unfairly, playing favorites among subordinates), belittling subordinates (yelling as subordinates, criticizing subordinates in front of others, embarrassing subordinates), using a forceful style of conflict resolution (forcing others to accept his or her point of view, demanding to get his or her way, not taking no for an answer), exacting noncontingent punishment (being often displeased with work for no apparent reason, frequently reprimanding subordinates without any explanation why, often criticizing even when subordinates are performing well).[19] The scale also includes two reverse-coded subscales: lacking consideration (friendly and approachable, does little things to make it pleasant to be a member of the group) and discouraging initiative (encourages subordinates to participate in important decisions, trains subordinates to take more authority, and encourages initiative in group meetings). Absent a valid and reliable toxic leadership scale, such models of petty tyranny in organizations provide a means of measuring specific problematic leader behavior in organizations.

A number of useful and insightful studies also have been produced on "abusive supervision," a construct very similar to most definitions of toxic leadership. Management literature tends to define abusive supervision as "subordinates' perceptions of the extent to which supervisors engage in the sustained display of hostile verbal and nonverbal behaviors, excluding physical contact."[20] When it comes to supervisor–subordinate relationships, it is the perception by the subordinate that counts, and subjective perceptions equal reality when it comes to abusive supervision. Supervisors need not intend to abuse their subordinates and may act with the goals of the organization at heart, but if they are perceived as abusive the harm is done. To be considered abusive, the supervisor engages in a *sustained* pattern of hostility (which exempts the single troublesome exchange). This description rightly excludes physical contact because that would constitute battery, which crosses into the realm of criminal behavior.

The U.S. Army has included a description of toxic leadership in the recent doctrinal publication *Army Leadership* (ADRP 6-22):

Toxic leadership is a combination of self-centered attitudes, motivations, and behaviors that have adverse effects on subordinates, the organization, and mission performance. This leader lacks concern for others and the climate of the organization, which leads to short- and long-term negative effects. The toxic leader operates with an inflated sense of self-worth and from acute self-interest. Toxic leaders consistently use dysfunctional behaviors to deceive, intimidate, coerce, or unfairly punish others to get what they want for themselves. The negative leader completes short-term requirements by operating at the bottom of the continuum of commitment, where followers respond to the positional power of their leader to fulfill requests.[21]

The army description includes some themes from other constructs, including adverse effects on individuals and the organization, dysfunctional behaviors, and a reliance on coercion to accomplish goals.

The operational definition used in this book establishes toxic leadership as demotivational behavior that negatively impacts unit morale and climate.[22] The first element of the toxic leader syndrome is an apparent lack of concern for the well-being of subordinates. This is a subjective determination that hinges on a perception by subordinates that the supervisor is unconcerned about their welfare. It exists when subordinates perceive that they are merely a means to the supervisor's end. Toxic supervisors are often quite responsive to higher headquarters and superiors without consideration for the long-term health of the organization and the people in it. The second element is a personality or interpersonal style that negatively affects organizational climate. This element covers a wide range of potential behavior—just about any behavior on the part of the supervisor that drives down organizational climate is considered problematic. Climate can be thought of as how members feel about an organization and is a concept associated with morale. To determine the climate of the organization, consultation with its members is necessary, and climate can be measured with a variety of tailored survey questionnaires. A third element of the syndrome could be considered a magnifying factor: a conviction by subordinates that the leader is motivated primarily by self-interest. Human beings have an innate sense for when others are getting ahead at their expense, and they do not appreciate being taken advantage of for another's gain. Military subordinates tend to react less negatively to demanding or even interpersonally challenged supervisors if they perceive the boss to be selfless and committed to organizational goals. They might not appreciate the style, but they tend to be more tolerant when they perceive the supervisor as being motivated to achieve an important greater good. The perception of the contrary makes the climate much worse.

In one of the earliest explorations of the toxic leadership concept, Marcia Whicker identified a series of "mals" to describe toxic leaders: maladjusted, malcontent, malfunctioning, and sometimes malevolent.[23] She further typed them as the absentee leader, the busybody, the controller, the enforcer, the street fighter, and the bully.

The *absentee leader* is disengaged, remote, and not attuned to the organization, creating a leadership vacuum in his or her absence. These are the most benign type and can even be likable: they crave approval and avoid conflict. However, they create an environment that allows toxic subordinates to thrive and wreak havoc on the organization. Trustworthy subordinates may thrive under a form of benign neglect, but toxic subordinates can as well—they realize that their toxic behavior will go unchecked, providing them with an open field for power games and turf battles.

The *busybody* is energetic, hectic, and even frantic at times even while unfocused and active in manipulating public opinion and trafficking in rumors, which he or she freely propagates at all levels of the organization. They place themselves at the center of the workplace and manufacture incessant demands for information, failing to distinguish between productive and unproductive effort.

The *controller* craves power and certainty and needs to be involved in every aspect of making decisions. Because they are uncomfortable with delegation, controllers hoard information and resist involving others. They are prone to perfectionism and are perpetually unhappy with the performance of others. They are demanding and intolerant of disorder. Controllers lack a vision for the organization, but they are quite clear about how things should be done in a procedural sense. They can be small-minded and petty.

*Enforcers* are upwardly focused and single-mindedly responsive to superiors. They aren't necessarily inherently evil; rather, they tend to magnify the characteristics of their immediate superiors. If they work for good leaders, they can be accurate and attentive administrators; likewise, if they work for evil people, they will do evil things. Whicker compares enforcers to mafia hit men, and service members have a similar term: "hatchet men" or "hatchet women," who do the dirty work for the boss. They thrive when teamed with absentee leaders or street fighters.[24] They do not necessarily crave the number one job or seek the limelight, and they can be expected to perpetuate the status quo.

*Street fighters* can be charismatic and appreciate personal loyalty yet are intolerant of dissent and apt to be defensive and possibly vindictive when their interests are threatened. They build empires and protect their turf with little consideration for the long-term effect on the organization as a whole. Street fighters are self-deceptive, believing that their way is the right way and that those who disagree must be vanquished.

*Bullies* are angry, autocratic, authoritarian, and prone to outbursts characteristic of a lack of composure. They elevate themselves by tearing down others and as a result are the most malicious of the toxic leader types. They justify their behavior as being in the best interests of the organization, and they can appear hardworking despite casting a destructive wake of fear and foreboding. Bullies are often arrogant, mercurial, narcissistic, and seemingly self-assured. They are jealous of the accomplishments of others and readily take credit for the work of their subordinates. They are easily slighted and harbor resentment for real or perceived insults. They will take great pains to find opportunities for vengeance against perceived opponents.

Toxic leaders are sometimes superficial, grandiose, and deceitful. They seem to lack remorse and show few indications of empathy. They manage to rationalize their behavior and fail to accept responsibility for their actions. They are frequently impulsive, lack long-term goals, and demonstrate antisocial behavior and poor behavioral control. In short, they meet the description of psychopaths. Psychopaths are "cunning master manipulators, able to influence individuals into fulfilling their own selfish ends. They hide their true motivations and project carefully formed personas to capitalize on the needs, expectations, and naïveté of individuals useful to them. When finished with their victims, they move on."[25]

A study of corporate psychopathy in the United States indicated that some who score high on a scale for measuring psychopathic tendencies achieve considerable rank and status in their organizations.[26] On 360-degree assessments, they received high scores on communication ability, creativity, innovation, and strategic thinking and lower scores in the management style, team player, and leadership domains, suggesting that "impression management and the ability to present well can obscure or trump subpar performance and behaviors that are damaging to the organization."[27] Not all toxic leaders are psychopaths, but some have behavior consistent with the description. Interestingly, those who suffer under them rarely report them or seek official redress for their ill treatment. As a result these leaders go uncaught and unchallenged unless they engage in malfeasance or criminal behavior. Some subordinates may feel ashamed of being manipulated, and others may be too intimidated or fearful of reprisal to speak up. The victims are simply relieved when the psychopath targets someone else, thankful the attention has moved away.[28]

Robert Sutton, professor of management science and engineering at the Stanford Engineering School, colorfully insists on referring to toxic leaders as "assholes" and suggests that workplaces would benefit from following the "no asshole rule."[29] This rule suggests that brilliance in other aspects of one's life does not compensate for demeaning and arrogant behavior that undermines a healthy environment. That is sage advice when choosing team members, but in most military organizations service members are assigned rather than hired. Commanders might have some influence over a few key positions, but they typically have no veto power over most assignment decisions made by higher headquarters. They are expected to make the best of the resources given. Sutton's rule still has value in military organizations if interpreted as an admonition to readily address interpersonal failings that impact the unit despite some other valued aspect or contribution. As one of his colleagues put it, "Listen, I don't care if that guy won the Nobel Prize . . . I just don't want any assholes ruining our group."[30]

Sutton's two-stage test is useful for determining whether a person is acting like an asshole:

Test One: After talking to the alleged asshole, does the "target" feel oppressed, humiliated, de-energized, or belittled by the person? In particular, does the target feel worse about him or herself?

Test Two: Does the alleged asshole aim his or her venom at people who are *less powerful* rather than at those people who are more powerful?[31]

The second stage of the test points out a dynamic that is frequently observed in toxic leaders. They tend to be responsive and even obsequious to superiors while inflicting misery on subordinates. In other words, they tend to kiss up while kicking down. As a result, toxic leaders don't look so bad from the top down while their suffering subordinates wonder how the organization could be so callous as to intentionally inflict such treatment upon them.

A colleague once suggested that the phenomenon of superiors failing to recognize toxic leadership in subordinates is similar to the dynamics of monkeys in the trees of the rain forest. He explained that in the rain forest the sweetest and fastest ripening fruit is found in the uppermost branches. High-status monkeys therefore congregate in the top branches and relegate low-status monkeys to lower levels of the forest. When the high-status monkeys look down, they see bright and shining monkey faces beaming back at them. From the lower branches looking up, the view is much different and not nearly as pleasant. What you see apparently depends on where you sit. The higher one ascends in the organizational hierarchy, the more favorable one's interpretation of the organizational dynamics tends to be. As people move up the hierarchy in terms of rank and status, fewer superiors have the power to wreck their day. Higher status individuals mistake their relational experiences as characteristic of all levels of the organization, but lower status individuals see the organization in a much different light.

Only those who demonstrate a sustained pattern of toxicity over time earn the title of toxic. Just because supervisors may bark at subordinates or occasionally lose their temper does not necessarily mean they're destructive. Leadership, especially in military organizations, is a tough business. It sometimes requires telling people to do difficult things that they would rather not do. It also requires setting high standards and being willing to address deficiencies directly, without hesitation. Sometimes there is nothing quite so motivating as a well-acted display of anger by the boss, provided the technique is not overused. If leaders are doing their job, there will be occasions when they are likely to be considered assholes by some, but that need not be their default mode of operation.[32] An important difference between tough and toxic leaders is that tough driving leaders will sometimes be unappreciated by their subordinates but toxic leaders get stuck in asshole mode. Consider the supervisor who publicly demeans a follower in front of other subordinates. Such undermining behavior is demoralizing and poor form at best, and it could be a litmus test for toxicity. Praise is best given publicly; criticism is appropriately delivered in private.

New insights often come from reading old books. Aristotle pointed out that desirable behavior sits on a spectrum between extremes of excess and deficiency.[33] Thus, virtue lies in the golden mean between undesirable deficiency and equally undesirable excess. Consider, for example, the notion of courage. Personal courage is a good thing, especially for military leaders. A deficiency of courage is referred to as cowardice, and there is no virtue in that. An excess of courage could manifest as imprudent risk-taking or a foolhardy disregard of danger. It is a brave act for a paratrooper to jump out of an aircraft while in flight—but jumping without a parachute is just plain stupid. Applying Aristotle's golden mean to the discussion of toxic leadership suggests that a timid, unengaged leadership style by a person in a position of authority who needs to be liked all the time is not desirable. There is also little to be said for the backbiting, belittling boss from hell who heaps abuse on subordinates and turns the workplace into a place of misery. Good leadership sits somewhere in the golden mean in between.

## The Scope of Toxic Leadership

Just because a social phenomenon is troubling does not necessarily mean that it is widespread or worthy of organizational attention. When resources are limited, enterprise leaders ought to be judicious in applying time, money, and effort to solve intermittent problems. There is no shortage of problems to address in large and complex organizations like the military, especially when it has been stressed by over a decade of a high operational tempo. On the one hand, if toxic leadership is a rare occurrence, then it is lamentable and perhaps warranting additional study but is not necessarily worthy of much sustained effort. On the other hand, if toxic leadership is a frequent or widespread occurrence, then the problem is worthy of considerable attention and investment from those who have the power and authority to direct additional interventions.

Abusive supervision affects an estimated 13.6 percent of U.S. workers.[34] Surveys of American workers have indicated that 64 percent of respondents currently work with a toxic personality and 94 percent have worked with someone fitting that description during their career.[35] A study accessing a random sample of 6,500 registered nurses in an urban South Florida county indicated an abusive supervision rate of 46.6 percent.[36] Data collected from

800 workers in a cross section of industries indicated that respondents experienced incivility at rate of 96 percent, with 48 percent claiming uncivil treatment once a week and 10 percent reported witnessing incivility every day.[37] At a presentation on toxic leadership for approximately 150 banking executives, the participants were asked whether they had seriously considered leaving a job because of the way they were treated by their supervisors. The vote was unanimous: every hand went into the air, and some stood on their chairs waiving to add emphasis. The same question posed to military audiences has resulted in a positive response from about one-third to one-half of attendees, depending on the experience level of those at the presentation.

Sector-specific studies and general workplace research might not have much to say to the unique context of the military. Soldiers, sailors, airmen, and marines are highly socialized to a hierarchical and regimented environment. They might be less sensitive to influence-behavior that would be problematic for their civilian counterparts. However, the focus on leadership that is characteristic of military organizations represents a double-edged sword. The emphasis on leadership in professional military schools and courses provides a common understanding of what leadership should look like. At virtually every transition point in a service member's career there is some form of school, course, or preparatory event that is designed to prepare for the next level of responsibility. Typically such courses are progressive and sequential, building on prior knowledge and experience. Most of the time schools and courses must be completed before the service members assume a higher grade or key position. Selection for certain courses stands as an indicator of whether a service member has long-term future potential in the organization. Such investment in leader development infrastructure is unmatched by any other sector or industry in American society. That emphasis also sets up some expectations with regard to the kind of leadership behavior military personnel anticipate. When service members do not experience the good leadership espoused in military publications, the result can be a sense of disappointment and betrayal. Bad leadership stands out in stark contrast to what they have come to expect. The military is a microcosm of the larger American society. Virtually every human phenomenon and proclivity represented in society at large can be expected to arise to some degree in military formations. The estimated rate of psychopathy in the general population is estimated at 1 percent, and one study suggested the rate in corporations is almost four times higher (3.9 percent).[38] The rate of psychopathy in military organizations is an open question.

A study that sampled students from all services in attendance at one of the war colleges indicated that all respondents had some experience with destructive leadership behaviors; 57.1 percent indicated that they had seriously considered leaving their service or agency due to poor treatment at the hands of a supervisor, and 17.7 percent indicated that the offending incident had occurred less than a year prior.[39] The fact that they had experience with toxic leadership is not surprising. War college students typically have between nineteen and twenty-one years of service. They have been around the block a few times and have served under varied supervisors. The fact that almost 18 percent were treated badly enough in the twelve months before entering the war college to consider leaving is surprising when you consider that their supervisors represent the highest echelons of the military and senior executive service. The supervisors of the war college sample are colonels and above—the very best that the Department of Defense can produce. They have made it through every gate and selection board. The study participants were given four narrative descriptions ranging from very favorable to toxic and were asked to place the general officers and members of the senior executive service that they were personally familiar with into each category. Respondents reported that 11 percent of their supervisors were viewed unfavorably and about 8 percent they considered toxic.

It is important to note that those selected to attend the war colleges are considered high-performing, high-potential officers and civilians. They have successful careers and were treated relatively well by their respective institutions. They have what can be described as "enriched jobs" that provide meaningful work, opportunities for growth, and autonomy. Subordinates with more enriched jobs are less impacted by destructive leaders.[40] Therefore, the occurrence of toxic leadership in that group would be expected to be lower than that experienced by senior military personnel at large.

The war college study was repeated at the U.S. Army Command and General Staff College to see whether there were similar patterns among midgrade officers.[41] More than half (61 percent) indicated that they had seriously considered leaving the service because of the way they were treated by their supervisors, and they noted that 18 percent of their supervisors fell in the toxic category. Members of the class were asked to identify the behaviors that were particularly problematic. The hit parade of offending leader behaviors was similar to that of the war college students: having a superior or arrogant attitude, relying on authority, unreasonably holding subordinates accountable for matters beyond their control, wanting things done the supervisor's way or no way, valuing his or her career over the good of the organization, losing his or her temper, playing favorites, administering policies unfairly, criticizing subordinates in front of others, claiming credit for the work of others, and ignoring required counseling activities were at the top of the list.

Leadership studies scholars have historically focused on leader tasks and behaviors through job analyses that identify specific tasks required at various levels of the organization.[42] Job analytic approaches can be helpful in identifying competency lists for developing curriculums in military schools and courses and for delineating tasks associated with officers, noncommissioned officers, and enlisted members. Only recently have studies begun to focus on the quality and impact of influence-behaviors. An example can be found in the Center for Army Leadership Annual Survey of Army Leadership, which provides a large, randomly selected, representative sample of officers, warrant officers, and army civilians. It is interesting to note that junior enlisted soldiers were not included in the sample, so when it comes to toxic leadership they remain largely unstudied.

Because the Center for Army Leadership survey has been conducted since 2005, it provides an opportunity to identify trends in important factors such as quality of leadership and indicators of destructive leadership. The 2012 survey indicated that most subordinates viewed their supervisors favorably, but 13 percent were classified as nonperforming (questionable potential for improvement, or failing to meet most basic expectations). The junior noncommissioned officers tended to classify a higher percentage of their supervisors as low or nonperforming.[43] Aggregating the "non-performing" and "low-performing" overall statistics resulted in an unfavorable subordinate opinion rate of over 30 percent, a number that the Center for Army Leadership described as encouraging, but others might interpret as alarming. The study did not use a measure of toxic leadership but did identify some commonly displayed negative leadership behaviors including setting misplaced priorities that interfere with accomplishing goals (19 percent), doing little to help his/her team to be more cohesive (18 percent), blaming other people to save himself/herself embarrassment (16 percent), and berating subordinates for small mistakes (16 percent).[44] Platoon sergeants and squad/section team leaders, an important level of first-line direct supervision, had the least favorable scores based on the ratings by their subordinates.

Information on leadership quality is not readily available from the other services, but if the army data are representative of the navy, marine corps, and air force as well, there is solace in knowing that there is more good leadership than bad, and it is reassuring that most subordinates see their leaders as effective. Military leadership doctrine is sound and useful for a unique and demanding context. The data reflect that there is work to be done with regard to ineffective leaders and those who engage in negative leadership behavior because toxic leadership at the hands of an abusive supervisor is still not a rare experience in the military.

Although toxic leadership is defined in different ways, there are some converging themes that emerge from the existing literature. Toxic leaders are interpersonally challenged, lack self-awareness, and treat others in ways that are not in the long-term best interests of world-class organizations like the military. They can manifest a range of problematic behaviors, from an absentee laissez-faire approach to a bullying authoritarian micromanaging style. There are a variety of identifiable toxic leadership types. It is not a single behavior that marks a supervisor as toxic but a pattern of sustained behavior over time that deserves the label. It is the perception of the targets of influence that is most important in determining toxic leadership, not the expressed intentions of those in authoritative positions. Some leaders of this type may be remorseless psychopaths who value personal gain at any cost, but many are dedicated to the organization and tireless in accomplishing the mission. A focus on short-term objectives and single metrics of success serves to mask toxic leadership behavior, and a focus on accomplishing tasks without regard for how those tasks are accomplished provides ample opportunity for toxic leadership to grow. Most supervisors in the military are not toxic, and military doctrine and publications are helpful in describing what good leadership should look like, but an exclusively positive view of leadership is misplaced and detracts from behavior that needs corrective action.

It is not hard to find toxic leadership. Most military personnel have experienced it at one time or another. There is no consensus as to how much toxic leadership is too much, but when it does occur it represents a violation of the unwritten contract with the American people about how their sons and daughters should be treated while in service to the nation.

# 2 Impact of Toxic Leadership

> You do not lead by hitting people over the head—that's
> assault, not leadership.
> —Dwight D. Eisenhower

Toxic leadership is an unfortunate part of the landscape in the profession of arms, an occurrence to be expected from time to time. The phenomenon would not be of much concern if the impact were inconsequential. After all, if service members are real professionals, dedicated to the task at hand and committed to mission accomplishment, does it really matter if they have a bad boss? Military culture emphasizes duty, a moral responsibility and obligation to perform regardless of the quality of leadership from superiors. Military personnel perform duties in austere, dangerous environments. They are intimately familiar with misery, danger, and hardship. Although high morale might be viewed as beneficial, happiness is not necessarily a requirement for mission accomplishment. If soldiers, sailors, airmen, and marines are duty bound to get the job done in spite of their supervisors, what is the cost of toxic leadership and why should we care?

Leadership is a big idea that transcends several academic disciplines. The study of leadership as we know it is a rather recent development, emerging predominately from the fields of history, political science, psychology, and management. Biographical studies were the norm for many years during an era where leadership was viewed largely from the perspective of great men. The nineteenth-century philosopher Thomas Carlyle famously asserted, "the history of what man has accomplished in this world, is at bottom the history of great men who have worked here."[1] It was a rather deterministic approach that favored traits and characteristics predisposing some to greatness. As to the development of leadership the approach had little to say, but it did provide inspirational examples. Leadership, however, is not limited to the great and mighty, nor is it restricted to men. Political science has favored the examination of specific leaders in key institutional settings such as the presidency. It also has tended to be leader-centric with less attention of the crucial role of followers, aside from voters. The advent of managerial sciences and psychology heralded the examination of leadership skills, behavior roles, and processes.

Today most scholars of acknowledge the phenomenon of leadership as an influence process. Joseph Rost, a pioneer in the field of leadership studies, defined leadership as "an influence relationship among leaders and followers who intend real changes that reflect their mutual purposes."[2] From Rost's perspective, leaders and followers are of equal value, and what designates a leader is not necessarily positional authority. Anyone can be a leader or follower, and those places may change frequently. For the situation to qualify as leadership, followers and leaders engage in a mutual agreement that constitutes a relationship. Power wielding and coercion that put others in a position of subservience do not qualify as leadership. That perspective, as with most contemporary leadership constructs, puts the process of leadership outside of formal positions: it might be helpful to hold a position, but those without formal authority or position can and do lead. From this perspective, followers and leaders are both important, and the relationship between the two is paramount.

Leader-member exchange theory (LMX) is an approach that focuses squarely on the quality of the relationship between leaders and followers. At its essence, LMX is interested in the ways that high-quality relationships—characterized by a high degree of trust, respect, and obligation—can be developed to result in desired organizational outcomes. Effective leadership fosters strong working relationships where both leaders and followers exert considerable influence on each other, more resembling a partnership than a traditional hierarchical arrangement.[3] In-groups and out-groups tend to form in organizations for a variety of reasons. Some members might have prior history with the boss or may be more favored due to perceptions of competence or loyalty. Supervisors might think they are treating everyone the same and have the intention of doing so, but it is only human to have an affinity for one person over another. Those affinities have implications for group dynamics.

Kathy Pelletier found a relationship between how leader behavior is perceived and the degree to which followers are part of an in-group or out-group.[4] In-group members typically have strong relationships with the leader and are perceived as dependable and competent, while out-group members have a more tenuous relationship with the leader and are not viewed as favorably. The latter have less frequent interactions with their supervisors than their in-group coworkers. Out-group members in organizations tend to know who they are, and in some cases they are acutely aware that they are not part of the inner circle. In Pelletier's experimental study, both in and out-group members tended to agree about what constituted toxicity, but when in-group members observed a toxic exchange they tended to see it as less problematic than members of out-groups did.[5]

This could explain why members of the civilian workforce and members of the reserve components perceive higher levels of toxicity than their active duty counterparts.[6] When a subordinate has a close working relationship with a superior that includes a history of care and high regard, the occasional outburst by the boss does not tend to have a lasting impact. Because the subordinate is confident in their relationship, things smooth over pretty quickly. In contrast, when a member of an out-group experiences a similar event, there is greater intensity and duration of impact. For example, when two military retirees discussed their perceptions of a supervisor they had both worked for, one of the former soldiers expressed strong opinions that the supervisor was toxic, an opinion many had shared. The other, who had been part of the supervisor's inner circle and a trusted confidant, had a completely different perception and cited many initiatives that had served the members of the command. In-group and out-group perceptions can vary significantly, and when it comes to leader–member relationships objective reality is less important than the perceptions of followers.

Psychologist Abraham Maslow is best known for his theory of human motivation, which posits the existence of stages of human growth, ranging from physiological needs such as air, food, and water to self-actualization where people reach the full realization of their potential.[7] In each stage, humans are motivated to engage in behavior and to associate with others in order to achieve their needs. When a lower stage has been achieved, the needs of the next higher stage become preponderant. Most in the military have their physiological needs met and are focused on needs somewhere between safety, ego, and self-actualization. Because the modern U.S. military is an all-recruited force, additional attention to what motivates men and women to join the military and stay beyond their initial enlistment is appropriate.

### The 4-F Theory of Affiliation

Think about why an individual chooses to voluntarily affiliate with organization A versus organization B. Why do they choose to work, worship, or associate with one organization over another? The four Fs are a way to frame our thinking about what motivates us to affiliate.

The first F represents *funds* or everything tangible received in return for associating with a particular organization. That includes salary, benefits, and perquisites. Money is an important motivator because it is the means by which most of the things necessary for physiological well-being are obtained in modern-day society. When there are insufficient funds to pay the mortgage or buy groceries, money becomes an overwhelming focus. Although funds are necessary, they are insufficient as a sole motivator for most people. People are capable of altruistic behavior and will sometimes act in self-sacrificial ways that do not make sense from a purely economic standpoint. They do not always affiliate with organizations that offer the highest pay. When made aware of another organization that does similar work at a higher salary, most will at least consider moving to the more lucrative offer, but not everyone makes the change. In fact, salary is rarely the primary driver for those in the nonprofit, government, and military sectors of society. Historically the American military has operated in a cycle of feast and famine. The military is lavished with appropriations during periods of armed conflict, but eyes turn to deficits in times of peace. Operation Enduring Freedom, which encompassed worldwide combat missions after the terrorist attacks of September 11, 2001, officially ended on December 27, 2014. On that same day, the *Army Times* headline read, "In 2015, Army Will Lose Nearly 20,000 Soldiers in Drawdown."[8] On December 30 another headline heralded, "DoD Braces for Political Battle over Military Pay."[9] The education and retirement benefits that seem appropriate during wartime appear excessively generous during peacetime. Fortunately for the military, a significant number of human beings are motivated by more than just wealth accumulation and are not as economically driven as some might suggest.

The second *F* represents *fun*, a frequently overlooked source of motivation in many organizations. A social wage is associated with having a good time. People are likely to remain with an organization despite economic incentives to go elsewhere if they are enjoying themselves. A news story about IDEO, one of the world's most successful design firms, highlighted a designer who had turned down medical school three times because he was having too much fun at the company.[10] There are many aspects of the military that are great fun. Jumping out of airplanes, operating high-performance equipment, firing sophisticated weapons systems, blowing stuff up, and testing one's physical and mental limits can be quite enjoyable. Applying a set of skills that were learned through rigorous preparation can be fun, and hard fought victories bring a sense of accomplishment. The military lifestyle attracts adventurous people, so there is often no shortage of good humor and even hilarity for those with a modicum of a sense of humor. *Reader's Digest* has published a long-running collection of jokes and stories about life in the military in its column "Humor in Uniform," which has provided laughs to readers for decades. Excessive deployments are taxing, but military personnel have a strong sense of mission that can be harder to find during peacetime: a 2014 survey of 2,300 active duty troops conducted by *Military Times* indicated declining morale, lower job satisfaction, diminished respect for their superiors, and a declining interest in re-enlistment.[11]

The third *F* stands for *fellowship*, the bonds of social and task cohesion that are often present in military organizations. Camaraderie, friendship, and affection for one's associates can drive extraordinary behavior. When military personnel work together under dangerous conditions they tend to establish close ties and bonds of friendship, trust, and even affection. The Medal of Honor was awarded posthumously to Ross McGinnis who sacrificed himself for fellow soldiers by covering a grenade that was thrown into his vehicle while on patrol in Iraq.[12] Such remarkable actions are not motivated by a paycheck—they come from within. Valor and sacrifice are part of the ethos of the military, and soldiers fight and die for those on their right and left. The bonds established in combat or intense military training often last far beyond the tenure of military service, and the presence of an external threat can serve as a catalyst that bonds very different people into a cohesive unit. It stands to reason that having shared experiences that are so foreign to the civilian populace lead those who leave the military to seek out others who understand what they have been through. Veterans' service organizations and military reunions provide a forum where such bonds can be renewed.

The fourth *F* is the *feeling* that the individual is part of something bigger than self. It is associated with a fundamental need to contribute, to leave a legacy, or make a difference. It is not enough for most human beings to simply live, consume, procreate, and die. They seek a sense of meaning and purpose, the pursuit of which can be highly motivating just as its achievement can be quite gratifying. Military service is perceived by many to be a noble endeavor, appreciated by the public. Aside from the obvious appreciation for their role as protectors of society, military personnel are perceived as personifying a number of admirable traits and attributes including loyalty, selfless sacrifice, discipline, and devotion to duty. A 2006 Korn/Ferry International report noted that military officers are overrepresented among the ranks of corporate chief executive officers.[13] The leadership skills learned in the military translate especially well to the boardroom:

- Working as part of a team.
- Organizing and planning effective use of resources.
- Communicating well.
- Defining goals and motivating others to pursue them.
- Maintaining highly developed ethics.
- Remaining calm under pressure.

In a popular Anheuser-Busch commercial that aired during the Super Bowl in 2005, a busy airport suddenly comes alive with a steady crescendo of applause as a group of service members dressed in camouflage and carrying military-issue backpacks files through the terminal. The soldiers are surprised by their reception, but they smile in response and some shake the hands of their admirers. The scene closes as the words "Thank You" appear on the screen. Such accolades are more prevalent in wartime. When the guns fall silent, thoughts inevitably turn to peace dividends and other domestic priorities. Drawdowns and reductions in force are decidedly unappreciated by those who want to remain in uniform but many are told their services are no longer necessary. For the rest, contrived training scenarios replace combat operations, flight hour allocations diminish, and finding parts to fix vehicles becomes increasingly difficult. The patriotic commercials and concerts for the troops are replaced by slick recruiting campaigns designed to appeal to specific demographics of the citizenry.

At the organizational level, especially in a postconflict military, the four Fs are worthy of serious consideration for recruiting and retaining talented people. Humans have highly varied motivations that can change over time; however, when faced with insufficient pay, no sense of attachment to others, and joyless and meaningless work, most would view the only rational course to be finding something else to do. It would be economically irrational to remain with an organization where all four Fs are in low supply. If there is a deficit in even one of the four Fs, a wise organization emphasizes the others to compensate and to encourage good people to remain.

In governmental organizations pay adjustments are not within the power of most supervisors. Although there may be some opportunities for bonuses for members of the civilian workforce or early promotion for a limited number of especially meritorious service members, pay and allowances are constrained and frequently lower than in the private sector. Subordinates are even less likely to indicate satisfaction with pay and allowances when they must work for a bad boss. Fun, fellowship, and feeling are intangibles that are directly influenced by leader behavior. Military leaders have an important role in establishing the conditions that make fun, fellowship, and feeling a reality. Leaders, through their interpersonal style, can make life in the unit enjoyable, and they can reinforce the bonds of fellowship. Supervisors can express appreciation and gratitude for subordinates in way that reinforces a sense of meaning and purpose. Conversely, a leader can make life miserable, take their subordinates' service for granted, and can unravel the bonds of fellowship through techniques such as excessive competition. It is no fun to work for a toxic leader, and working for one has a deleterious impact on many aspects of quality of life. Those working for toxic leaders report less satisfaction with their relationships, not only with their supervisors but with their coworkers and subordinates as well. Pain and suffering tend to obscure meaning and purpose, and it can be hard to focus on societal contribution or the inherent nobility of a task when suffering under a toxic supervisor.

An air force lieutenant colonel selected for early promotion to colonel made the decision to retire rather than accept promotion after suffering abusive and demeaning treatment from a major general.[14] He cited as his reason for retiring the impact of work stress on his health and marriage. The influence of toxic leadership extends into families and relationships beyond the boundaries of the workplace. Before retiring, he initiated an inspector general complaint that substantiated a pattern of frequent abuse as well as cruel and oppressive behavior. The general went through front office personnel at an unusually high rate; high turnover is not always an indicator of toxic leadership, but it was apparent in this case. As one subordinate stated, "I've seen a lot of good and bad leadership styles in my career, but he is just down, downright mean . . . I believe he got to the place he got because he gets results. Unfortunately he gets results on the backs of the people that work for him."[15] Callous disregard for the welfare of subordinates is a key indicator of toxic leadership. Another witness stated that he was "the worst I've seen. [His leadership] did not follow the 'servant leadership model,' and he created a repressive environment."[16] That comment reflects the expectation of a particular kind of positive leadership style where those in charge are in service to the goals and objectives of the organization and the people in it. Talent tends to flee toxicity.

## What Research Says about the Impact of Toxic Leadership and Similar Constructs

Disrespectful treatment that is characteristic of toxic leadership is a "social toxin" that "paralyzes its victims, draining energy, initiative, and desire while undermining their physical and psychological well-being."[17] The estimated annual cost of abusive supervision from increased absenteeism, turnover, and decreased effectiveness exceeds 23.8 billion dollars.[18] Porath and Pearson polled eight hundred managers and employees throughout the United States and Canada in seventeen industries to determine the reactions of those who were on the receiving end of incivility:

- 48 percent intentionally decreased their work effort.
- 47 percent intentionally decreased the time spent at work.
- 38 percent intentionally decreased the quality of their work.
- 80 percent lost work time worrying about the incident.
- 63 percent lost work time avoiding the offender.
- 66 percent said that their performance declined.
- 78 percent said that their commitment to the organization declined.
- 12 percent said that they left their job because of the uncivil treatment.
- 25 percent admitted to taking their frustration out on customers.[19]

If the productivity impact Porath and Pearson documented in civil society is mirrored in military organizations then it is a problem that is worthy of additional attention.

An analysis of the crash of a B-52 that killed the pilot and crew at an air show demonstration was prefaced with a sage observation: "When leadership fails and a command climate breaks down, tragic things can happen."[20] During an air show a pilot engaged in maneuvers that exceeded the capacity of the aircraft by banking past 90 degrees, whereupon it stalled, struck a power line, and crashed. An extensive investigation painted a useful picture of the event and the factors that had contributed to the tragedy. The pilot had arrogantly overestimated his own abilities and the capabilities of his aircraft, and he had seemed immune to input from his subordinates. Some crewmembers had refused to fly with the veteran pilot, even under orders. Subordinates knew there was a problem, but apparently he didn't look so bad from the top down. Superior officers had failed to address the pilot's previous flight safety violations and had not acted on complaints from subordinates about reckless flying. Toxic leaders thrive under such laissez-faire leadership styles that leave them free to their own destructive devices. The hesitation to intervene had permitted a bad situation to grow even worse, with tragic consequences. There were a number of factors that contributed to the crash, but an environment where subordinates felt uncomfortable bringing bad news to the boss is worthy of mention. Frank and honest information does not tend to easily flow up and down the chain of command when toxic leadership is present.

Many who experience abusive supervision, especially those who are at lower levels of an organization, are more likely to leave their jobs, and those who remain report lower levels of job satisfaction, life satisfaction, commitment to the organization, and higher levels of work-to-family conflict, family-to-work conflict, depression, anxiety, and emotional exhaustion.[21] The negative impact on retention is a priority concern for the military in times of personnel shortage. Military recruiting can be a business of boom and bust, impacted by the strength of the economy and availability of good jobs, so the services are sometimes driven to examine reasons for the occasional exodus of midgrade officers. When turnover is high, leadership is usually identified as a factor. Job mobility seems to attenuate to some degree the impact of abusive supervision; such situations tend to be less stressful when subordinates can separate themselves from their supervisors or have the option of leaving the organization. That is a good thing for military populations where moves are frequent, but escape from toxic leaders is usually not something military personnel can invoke upon demand. Unlike those working in the private sector who can quit and thereby exit a bad situation, military personnel are constrained by assignment policies, service obligations, and terms of enlistment.

A meta-analysis of fifty-seven studies on the extent of the impact of bad leaders indicated that followers of destructive leaders tend to have negative attitudes about their supervisors and are likely to direct resistance and retaliation toward them.[22] Those who suffer under destructive leaders have negative attitudes about not only their jobs but also the organization as a whole. For example, the commanding officer of a Ticonderoga class guided missile cruiser was removed after an inspector general investigation substantiated behavior *Time* described as "the closest thing the U.S. Navy had to a female Captain Bligh."[23] The captain's pattern of humiliating and belittling verbal abuse had led to an environment of fear and hostility on the cruiser. Recall that toxic leaders tend to be ineffective in developing and mentoring subordinates: subordinates who sought her help were rebuffed, and in a characteristic display of lack of composure, she reportedly would throw items including ceramic cups at her officers in fits of anger. She was apparently well known for this pattern of behavior, yet she still had been elevated to a position of great responsibility. At a previous assignment, when her replacement was announced the sailors onboard reportedly cheered in celebration. Though her behavioral style was well known to those who worked for her, those observations were not being captured in fitness reports. As is characteristic of toxic leaders, she demonstrated a remarkable lack of self-awareness by appearing surprised at the allegations and maintaining that her intent was simply to maintain very high standards. Toxic leaders often have good intentions yet fail to recognize the negative impact they have on their subordinates. She believed a small group of disgruntled officers was undermining her with the crew; she felt her leadership style emphasized the seriousness of her concerns and helped to "pressurize the situation."[24] Thus she rationalized her behavior and externalized the problem, laying the blame at the feet of those she saw as disloyal officers. Toxic leaders with a narcissistic bent frequently expect loyalty from subordinates but do not necessarily give it to those they perceive as beneath them. Most subordinates do not initiate formal complaints in response to toxic leadership out of fear of retribution, a sense of loyalty, or simply hope for better days to come. In this case, the investigation was initiated after numerous anonymous complaints.

Those who serve under toxic leaders tend to blame the organization for placing toxic leaders over them, and they resent the lack of intervention that keeps them there. Such attitudes result in higher levels of turnover and counterproductive work behavior. The impact of toxic leadership extends well beyond the boundaries of the workplace to include increased levels of stress and decreased well-being. As an example, employees managed by abusive supervisors are significantly more likely to report drinking problems.[25] More generally subordinates tend to react to toxic leaders in one of two ways: escape or emulation.

The first reaction involves an attempt to escape the destructive sphere of influence. Suffering subordinates can escape at the end of their enlistment period by exiting the service, but there are frequently other options available to military personnel including transfer, schooling, and deployment. The second fundamental reaction is to view the toxic leader as a role model under the assumption that since the organization has rewarded the leader with additional rank and responsibility, destructive behavior must be the pathway to success. Thus, toxic leaders can replicate themselves in organizations, a phenomenon that is especially problematic when we understand that supervisors tend to rate more favorably those who are similar to them. We all tend to react favorably when we see aspects of our own personality and approach that we can identify with in others. When toxic leadership styles become accepted as a pathway to success, the problem begins to resemble a viral infection that spreads throughout the body of an organization.

The pernicious effects of toxic leaders are well established in the general leadership, psychology, and management literature, but studies focusing on military populations are less common. Even though the focus on military populations is still emerging, there have been a number of useful studies that suggest the negative impact of toxic leaders should be of concern to those who see the importance of a healthy and effective military.

The 2012 Center for Army Leadership Annual Survey of Army Leadership (CASAL) validated several of the relationships suggested by non-military research.[26] When army leaders demonstrated core competencies and attitudes associated with good leadership, the result was a positive effect on cohesion, discipline, subordinate motivation, work quality, commitment to the organization, and confidence in following the superior into life-or-death situations.[27] Other leader behaviors were shown to hinder the development of trust, including displays of favoritism, unequal treatment, or partiality; lack of character; self-interest or self-concern; lack of competence, benevolence, or support; and negative leadership in general as demonstrated by retribution, intimidation, ineffectual leadership, and micromanagement.[28] There is a positive correlation between trust and subordinates' psychological well-being. Those who rated their immediate supervisor high in building trust also reported higher levels of their own well-being.[29]

A study of abusive supervision among national guard members and their supervisors established a relationship between abusive supervision and organizational citizenship behavior.[30] Organizational citizenship behavior is action by an employee that extends beyond the requirements of the position. It includes discretionary acts that are in the interests of the organization—in other words, going the extra mile. For example, consider walking across the unit area and discovering an item of litter a few feet off of the sidewalk. There is no one else in the vicinity, and it would be easy to simply pretend not to see the offending item and walk by. Organizational citizenship behavior is represented by taking the few extra steps to pick up the litter and dispose of it in a trash can. Soldiers tend to engage in organizational citizenship behavior at a lower rate when experiencing abusive supervision. Soldiers are more likely to merely comply with orders and less likely to engage in the extra effort that comes from commitment. Some abused subordinates continue to engage in organizational citizenship behavior because they feel such behavior is inherent in the job—a reflection of a sense of duty and obligation to the unit, reflecting the power of fellowship and feeling. The work of today's military is difficult and challenging to the degree that mere compliance with orders is no substitute for commitment.

A 2009 study conducted at the Army War College examined the impact of toxic leadership on senior military officers and civilians, focusing on lieutenant colonels and colonels from all services as well as civilians at the grades of GS14 and GS15.[31] That study found an inverse relationship between destructive leadership and satisfaction. Virtually every measure of satisfaction was negatively impacted when working for a bad supervisor, including supervisor relationships, direction received from superiors, pay and benefits, promotion opportunities, work, the job as a whole, coworker relationships, and subordinate relationships. Even senior officers experience toxic leadership, and they are not immune to its negative impact. The presence of toxic leadership was a significant predictor of dissatisfaction, but for this career-oriented population it was not a predictor of departure despite the fact that many of them were retirement eligible or would be in just a few years. Only one of the 174 respondents indicated that it was highly unlikely that he or she would remain in service.[32]

Apparently senior military personnel suffer under toxic leaders as well, but they do not necessarily flee their influence. Several explanations are possible for this finding, including the fact that senior military personnel are "all in": their professional and personal identities are interwoven. To some degree, what they do is who they are. They also have experienced a wide range of leadership behaviors in the course of a career and are not as put off by a bad boss as those with less experience. They know there is more good leadership than bad in the military, and that provides them some perspective. That they were part of a small group of their peers selected for the war college was a signal to them that they are valued by the organization and have potential for higher levels of responsibility. It takes more than a bad boss to derail them from their professional goals.

To test whether that dynamic holds at lower grades, the study was repeated with majors at the U.S. Army Command and General Staff College. Unlike the more senior war college class, midgrade officers were significantly less likely to remain in service if they had experience with toxic leadership. Those officers with ten years or less experience who worked for toxic leaders tended to look for an exit. Most of the military research on the topic has focused on officer populations, and additional work is warranted to establish the scope, nature, and impact of toxic leadership with enlisted populations.

A recent study established a statistically significant relationship between toxic leadership and cynicism, a factor in employee burnout, emotional exhaustion, and turnover.[33] Research conducted at the U.S. Air Force Academy found evidence that cadets who perceived their commanding officers as exhibiting higher levels of toxic leadership (abusive supervision, authoritarian leadership, narcissism, self-promotion, and unpredictability) were more cynical about their organization as a whole. Self-promotion was the leader behavior most predictive of organizational cynicism. Those who are cynical find it difficult to trust, and they assume malevolent intent in the motives of others. Once trust has been betrayed and cynicism takes hold, it can be quite difficult to reestablish a positive leader–follower dynamic.

A large-sample study of soldiers in Iraq (2,572 participants) found abusive supervision negatively impacted moral courage and identification with organizational values.[34] That study is of particular importance because it is one of the few that has been conducted in a war zone, where the organizational effectiveness of a military organization is ultimately decided. Those who reported experience with abusive supervisors or saw abusive behavior directed toward their peers also reported witnessing higher levels of unethical acts. They were also less likely to report the ethical transgressions of others. Perhaps those who witnessed abusive supervision were less likely to report unethical activity because of a lack of confidence in their chain of command. Those who are beset with cynicism might be less attached to organizational values and see the reporting of unethical acts as futile or even risky if it were to draw the ire of an abusive supervisor. The study found higher levels of moral courage and identification with organizational values among those who had experienced lower levels of abusive supervision. It is no surprise that protracted combat is morally corrosive to military units, but the study identified leadership style as an important factor in maintaining an ethical unit climate in a war zone. There is significant reliance in the military on the notion of character, but it appears that situational and contingent variables such as leader behavior are also important drivers of ethical or unethical conduct.

It is possible to become trapped under a toxic leader in a way that leads to a sense of helplessness and despair. Cultural Anthropologist David "Doc" Matsuda was asked to look into the rise in military suicides while he was serving as a cultural advisor in Iraq.[35] He conducted extended, open-ended interviews with fifty personnel who had been associates of eight soldiers who had committed suicide. He focused on the circle of trust and those closest to the suicides to better understand the social context surrounding the incidents. In his 2010 report, Matsuda concluded that in all eight cases toxic leadership was either a contributing factor or a precipitating event. The dynamics of toxic leadership that led to a sense of hopelessness among the presuicidal soldiers had begun with their reception in their units as newcomers. Because individual shortcomings have group consequences, the incoming soldiers had received warnings to avoid screwing up from the more experienced members of the group. Their supervisors had tended to withhold their support from the newcomers until they had proved themselves as competent and contributing members of the team. Their peers also avoided the newcomers, happy to no longer be the "new guys" themselves; the arrival of new, lower status members had effectively provided the others with a status elevation within the group while their supervisor's attention focused on the unproven members of the team. Seeking the favor of higher-ranking officers, the noncommissioned officers "smoked" the new soldiers through ridicule and moved those who did not meet expectations from one platoon to another. The transfers were not necessarily favorably received, and in some cases they were treated with disdain. The soldiers had viewed suicide not as a selfish act but as a means of control and escape—they tragically reasserted control of their destiny with their final act of self-destruction.[36]

Matsuda's observations are compelling and raise important questions about the relationship between leadership style and military suicide. Additional research is necessary, however, before establishing a direct link between suicide and toxic leadership. Although there is evidence to suggest that interpersonal relationships tend to unravel before a suicide attempt and that toxic leadership can be a factor in degrading those relationships, there are also many other intervening variables to consider in such a complex human dynamic. Preexisting mental health conditions, alcohol or drug consumption, family history, and situational factors such as access to weapons are also important considerations, just to name a few. It is important to remain circumspect about the power of one variable such as quality of leadership to drive an individual to suicide, especially in the military where leaders tend to be held accountable for all that happens in their units. Suicides do occur on the watch of even the most enlightened leaders, and not all who suffer under toxic leaders contemplate such a drastic solution. There are far too many suicides, but they are fortunately relatively rare occurrences in a statistical sense. Care should be taken when extrapolating from a small number of events.

Psychologist Philip Zimbardo has long been interested in the process by which otherwise good people engage in unethical behavior. His famous Stanford prison experiment demonstrated the power of role and situation in driving human behavior. In that experiment a group of graduate students were randomly assigned to roles as either prison guards or prisoners in a mock prison constructed in the basement of a campus building. The experiment had to be cancelled after five days when the behavior of some of the "guards" approached an unacceptable level of hostility (if not brutality) and the "prisoners" began manifesting symptoms of psychological harm. A similar pattern was observed at the now infamous Abu Ghraib Central Prison when military and civilian personnel engaged in the abuse of detainees. Zimbardo served as a witness for the defense at the court martial of the noncommissioned officer in charge of the night shift at Abu Ghraib. He identified a series of psychosocial cues and situational factors including fear, exhaustion, pressure to produce actionable intelligence, and the absence of mission-specific training that contributed to the debacle.[37] Reducing unethical behavior is of particular concern to military organizations, and now there is evidence that interventions to reduce toxic leadership are a means to retaining a more healthy and committed force.

Examples of toxic leadership in military organizations are not limited to those in uniform. An anonymous complaint to the army inspector general's office accused a civilian member of the senior executive service and assistant to the secretary of the army of belittling members of her staff, requiring them to get lunch for her on a daily basis, and requiring subordinates to purchase coffee and tea for her at their own expense.[38] She obviously failed to discern the difference between personal and organizational assets, leading her to misappropriate subordinates for the provision of personal services. Toxic leaders can be painfully self-centered, seeing subordinates as a mere means to their selfish ends. On one occasion she tasked a subordinate to take fourteen pairs of shoes to the Pentagon shoe repair shop for polishing or repair. Her perfectionist and authoritarian leadership style resulted in low morale, unnecessary tension, and disruption due to the high level of turnover as subordinates fled her management style. When another member of the senior executive service was asked whether he would work for her again, he replied, "Not on my worst day."[39] Although her office was recognized for producing excellent products for superiors, she complained publicly about her staff members, threatened and mentally abused her subordinates, frequently used sarcasm and the cold shoulder on some subordinates, and failed to provide work development for others. Superiors only saw her work product, and they failed to discern the negative impact she was having on organizational climate. When an investigator asked whether she saw a need for change, she indicated that other than using the staff for personal services she did not. "She believed that she empowered subordinates, strove to build a cohesive team, and did an enormous amount of work for her organization."[40] Many of her subordinates would only agree with the latter point—her work ethic was not in question. Her leadership style, however, was inappropriate. She apparently not only lacked self-awareness but also failed to perceive how her leadership style was impacting others, exhibiting a debilitating lack of emotional intelligence.

In many of the cases used to illustrate toxic leadership, the supervisors had extensive education and experience. They were promoted to demanding positions of great responsibility after having demonstrated exceptional skills and talents, and they seemed to have good intentions. Yet the toxic bosses managed to alienate their subordinates to such a degree that they took the remarkable step of filing official complaints that included sworn statements documenting abusive and improper behavior. In some cases toxic leaders were first called out for violating rules and regulations, but behind that was the festering level of discontent stemming from their subordinates' belief that they were treated cruelly or unfairly. Each of those accused of toxic leadership rationalized their behavior and either did not recall or arrogantly refuted specific incidents that had galled subordinates. The immediate supervisors of the toxic leaders failed to see the degree to which their subordinates' leadership style was harming the organization. Some supervisors of toxic leaders even appeared surprised by the allegations. The chain of command either did not see or did not act until the allegations had been fully documented by an independent investigation.

General David Perkins, who served as a brigade commander in combat and led the tank units that first entered Baghdad during Operation Iraqi Freedom, demonstrated an understanding of toxic leadership as an organizational problem while he commanded the army's Combined Arms Training Center. During a National Public Radio interview he said,

> If we don't do something about toxic leadership . . . not to be too dramatic, but it does have life or death consequences . . . I can just tell you from experience . . . that if you have toxic leadership, people will get sort of what we call the "foxhole mentality." They'll just hunker down and no one is taking what we call prudent risk . . . They're not being innovative, they're not being creative. And some people who are toxic leaders, they might be able to get some short-term results and get an immediate mission at hand done. But in the process, they are destroying the organization and destroying their people.[41]

The jury is in: not only is toxic leadership an all too frequent experience for those in uniform, but it also negatively impacts a host of positive variables, including satisfaction, cohesiveness, commitment, ethical conduct, and effectiveness. It frequently leads to an unhealthy unit climate that can result in dysfunction and even tragedy. Toxic leadership is not conducive to a world-class military in a democratic society, and especially not to an all-recruited force.

# 3 Creating and Sustaining Toxic Leaders

Rank does not confer privilege or give power. It imposes responsibility.
—Peter F. Drucker

Having established some knowledge of the scope, nature, and impact of toxic leadership, it is appropriate to derive some insight into why there are so many who exhibit a destructive leadership style and why they seemingly thrive in military organizations. Prevalent sociological phenomena usually serve some organizational purpose or provide benefit in a way that is not always apparent at first glance. Perhaps there are aspects of the military that incubate or sustain toxic leadership. "Destructive leadership cannot be understood without a full examination of the entire leadership process, and particularly the institutional and organizational crucibles in which it exists."[1] In other words, it is insufficient to merely study toxic leadership at the individual level of analysis. Leadership is a socially constructed concept enmeshed in a collective web of meaning. The environment in which individuals live and work—the organizational structures and culture—deserve some examination as contributors to the emergence of toxic leaders. Toxic leaders, susceptible followers, and conducive environments represent an unholy trinity that can lead to destructive outcomes.[2]

"Toxic leaders thrive only in a toxic system."[3] That might be a bit of an overstatement as toxic leaders can be found in almost any organization, but the observation that toxic leaders are agile operators and organizational chameleons who skillfully harness systems of power is on point. Destructive supervisors are capable of masking their toxicity and fostering special relationships with powerful protectors; they are careful about discerning those they can abuse from those they must be nice to.[4] Like Janus, the mythical Roman two-headed god, they present separate faces to the world—the face of a trusted and loyal subordinate who gets things done to their superiors and the face of a tyrant to subordinates. Here are six ways in which organizations promote toxicity:

1. The structure changes to accommodate the toxic personality.
2. The organization tolerates the toxicity, provided the individual is productive.
3. The team climate changes when the toxic person is present.
4. The organization's leaders are unaware of the toxic person's behavior.
5. Less productive team meetings are tolerated.
6. The organization contributes to the toxic person getting away with counterproductive behaviors.[5]

## Climate and Culture

Organizational culture and climate are two different but related constructs. Climate equates to how members feel about their organization. Climate is a relatively surface-level, temporary phenomenon subject to direct influence and fairly easily assessed through surveys and direct observation. Culture is much deeper, resulting from shared beliefs, values, and assumptions that are not as subject to direct control.[6] An experienced officer or non-commissioned officer can get a fairly accurate read on the climate of a unit after only a short amount of time. How members dress and speak about their unit, the state of the living areas, and even small things such as how salutes are exchanged provide subtle clues. The ethereal nature of climate can be illustrated with an example. Consider a high school sports team that has played well throughout the season and earned a shot at the state championship. Now imagine what the bus ride to the big game feels like: spirits are high, players are exuberant, and those associated with the team are full of expectation. Now imagine what the bus ride home feels like after they lose the championship game. The difference is palpable and easily discerned by even a casual observer. It doesn't take much to change the climate. Organizational culture, however, is enacted through social interaction over time. It also tends to emerge in unpredictable ways. Culture is a powerful force that has a life span longer than the term of most military leaders. In established organizations there is typically a culture in place before a leader arrives, and one that abides long after that leader departs. Leaders might be able to influence culture, but they do not control it.

Edgar Schein has provided a helpful definition of culture: "The culture of a group can now be defined as a pattern of shared basic assumptions learned by a group as it solved problems of external adaptation and internal integration, which has worked well enough to be considered valid and, therefore, to be taught to new members as the correct way to perceive, think, and feel in relation to those problems."[7] Culture becomes embedded into an organization, and because it is learned and shared behavior, it can be very resistant to change. Culture is what everyone in the organization seems to know without it ever appearing in handbooks or standard operating procedures. New members typically find out about the cultural norms and expectations when they inadvertently violate them. They get a reaction from other members that lets them know they are outside the boundaries of acceptable behavior.

When organizations are examined from a cultural viewpoint, attention is drawn to aspects of organizational life that historically have been ignored or understudied, such as the stories people tell to newcomers to explain "how things are done around here," the ways in which offices are arranged and personal items are or are not displayed, jokes people tell, the working atmosphere (hushed and luxurious or dirty and noisy), and so on.[8]

Culture can be tricky to diagnose because it is a deep-level phenomenon that is not apparent at first sight. Diagnosing culture is typically the work of anthropologists, who spend extended periods of time immersed in a group attempting to understand the nuances and meaning of social interactions. Diagnosing culture, as difficult as it is, can be child's play when compared to attempting to change it. Culture changes slowly, and despite the best of intentions it does not always emerge in a predictable fashion. Leaders who believe they can directly influence organizational culture are frequently disappointed. Surface level compliance and cosmetic changes do not necessarily reflect changes in underlying beliefs and assumptions. It can be easy to confuse the expression of culture through mission statements, office arrangements, rituals, and rights with more powerful implicit assumptions that people carry in their heads.[9]

Anthropologist Anna Simons spent over a year observing army special forces teams at Fort Bragg, North Carolina.[10] Despite a system of training and equipping that was virtually identical across teams, she identified very different worldviews and operating norms in two units within the same group. One team (ODA 309) valued and believed in hard work: "If the patrol route took the team through a swamp, everyone filed through the swamp. If the exercise required that the team stay tactical (no tents, lights, stoves, or amenities), the team stayed tactical."[11] The other team (ODA 300) valued cunning and would not hesitate to cheat as a group. For them, it was right as long as they did not get caught: "When members of this team went to the field they always tried to carry pillows. Whenever possible too, they would escape the field to carouse in town."[12] Both teams valued mission accomplishment and camaraderie, and both teams were operationally effective. Simons noted that all special forces teams had some common characteristics. They valued unconventional approaches, were adaptive, competitive, elite, and flexible, and they all sought excellence. Different teams, however, developed different subcultures. If one were to accept the cover story presented by command briefings and surface level observations, one would miss some very important differences. One advantage of thinking about organizational culture is that it drives interested observers and group members to a more sophisticated understanding of group dynamics.

Schein suggested a three-stage model for managing learning and culture change.[13] Step one involves unfreezing the current state that occurs when there is enough disconfirming data present to cause serious discomfort and disequilibrium, leading to anxiety and guilt. Threats to survival can produce a motivation to change if the anxiety produced by the threat exceeds the anxiety associated with having to learn new ways of doing things. Step two is the stage where the organization learns new concepts, new meanings for old concepts, and new standards of evaluation. There is typically a painful period of unlearning involving denial and resistance. A new way of thinking and working eventually emerges. During step three, the new learning is seated in organizational culture. Schein suggests this occurs when organizational members learn that the new ways work better and are perceived as successful enough to pass on to new members.

Cultures can be devilishly hard to change, at least in ways that leaders want them to. Culture changes when underlying values and belief structures change; they do not change because of directives from higher headquarters, even in a relatively obedient and disciplined organization like the military. Sometimes organizational members resist threats to deeply held assumptions and beliefs. Change at that level can be unsettling, especially when change is perceived as a challenge to tradition or powerful interests.

Resistance to culture change is not necessarily overt or militant. There are a thousand ways to appear to be compliant on the surface while quietly slow-rolling or undermining a change initiative. Hazing in the military through unofficial or semiofficial rites and rituals provides an illustration of the staying power of some practices despite exhortations of leaders and earnest measures to control or eliminate them. The common, if unauthorized, practice of awarding "blood wings" in parachute units by pounding insignia pins into the flesh has its equivalent in "blood stripes," which are bestowed in an equally brutal fashion. The navy's line crossing ceremony commemorating a sailor's first crossing of the Equator frequently descends into unauthorized corporal punishment and degrading activities that serve to mark the distinction between veteran "shellbacks" and the novice "pollywogs." Despite the most earnest pronouncements by senior leaders, including official policies in all services that outlaw hazing, such ceremonies remain a part of the military experience, and they frequently get out of hand. A search on the video-streaming site YouTube provides ample evidence that such hazing is not only alive and well but is considered acceptable enough to be posted on the Internet for all to see. Despite decades of efforts to stem binge drinking by military personnel, including draconian enforcement of penalties for intoxicated driving, excessive alcohol consumption remains prevalent among soldiers, sailors, airmen, and marines.

The need to belong is a powerful driver of human behavior, and individuals will sacrifice a great deal to obtain and maintain membership in a group. The willingness to endure outlandish and demeaning hazing rituals is evidence of the power of group membership. Service members are willing to undergo exceptionally painful and physically taxing trials to earn their way into elite units. The tribulations of basic underwater demolition school for navy SEALs, ranger school, and the special forces qualification course are but a few examples. Why should we be surprised that military personnel are willing to suborn toxic leaders in order to remain a part of the team? Once toxic leadership becomes a part of organizational culture, it can be hard to eradicate.

## Aspects of Military Culture That Can Lead to Toxic Leadership

Military personnel are typically relentlessly goal driven with a strong sense of mission. Once given an objective, they take great pride in accomplishing difficult jobs—even what might appear at first glance to be impossible. It is a culture and environment that values leaders who accomplish tasks under harsh and dangerous conditions. There is a tendency to accept and even glorify leaders who accomplish the mission even if their style of leadership is questionable. Such a single-minded focus on mission accomplishment is laudable, but it can also translate to a short-term perspective that neglects the long-term health and welfare of people. For example, by all accounts, a reserve signal battalion deployed to Iraq did a good job of accomplishing its assigned missions. They facilitated communications in theater and generally served those who depended on their services well. It was not until they redeployed that problems began to emerge. Noncommissioned officers reportedly engaged in creative and unauthorized means of punishing junior enlisted soldiers during the deployment, including the withholding of mail. There were multiple allegations of sexual and other misconduct by unit leaders, and the office of the inspector general was kept busy with a litany of complaints. Soldiers wanted out of the unit, reenlistments plummeted, and morale was exceptionally low. Thus, mission accomplishment alone is an insufficient metric for determining whether a unit is good. Attention to how the mission is accomplished is also important. Leaders who fail to consider the long-term impact of a high operational tempo can run the best of units into the ground.

Human social groups develop certain expectations about how leaders are supposed to look and act. Individuals who fit those preconceived notions are more likely to readily garner followers or be seen as leaders than those who do not. Military organizations seem to have a preference for leaders who are "large and in charge." Young officers are encouraged to seize the initiative with bumper-sticker exhortations such as "When in charge take charge" or "Lead, follow, or get out of the way." The archetypical military leader is charismatic, self-assured, extraverted, physically fit, and decisive. Bold, audacious, big personality field commanders in the style of Patton or MacArthur are more likely to be venerated than those in the more cerebral mold of Marshall or Eisenhower. An example of the preference for a certain archetype can be found in remarks attributed to the former commandant of the marine corps, General Alfred M. Gray, who "complained about 'too many intellectuals' at the top of the armed services. Naming no names, the 59-year-old Marine general said that what is needed is not intellectuals but 'old-fashioned gunslingers' who like a good fight and don't spend their time with politicians."[14] This military leadership archetype might serve to mask toxic leadership because there is a fine line between being self-assured and decisive and being autocratic or narcissistic.

Because of their strong sense of mission, military organizations are prone to a form of resource–mission mismatch whereby they willingly accept tasks or establish standards of success for which they are not properly manned, trained, or equipped. The previously mentioned Abu Ghraib detainee abuse scandal could serve as an example of how the desire to accomplish a mission outstripped the available resources. There is evidence from several investigative reports released to the public, including the Fay and Schlesinger reports, that the limited detainee facilities were overwhelmed by an influx of prisoners without a corresponding allocation of resources.[15] As the insurgency grew in Iraq in 2003, ninety military police soldiers from a poorly trained, weakly led military police brigade were tasked with securing Abu Ghraib Central Prison's seven thousand detainees.[16] Once the extent of detainee abuse was uncovered, extensive resources, including new leaders, engineer support, and ample personnel, were redirected to the prison.

Excellence is the watchword of many military organizations, and failure is not an option. That "let us try" and "give us something we can't do" attitude sometimes sets up no-win situations that lead to moral compromise, especially in organizations that depend upon inspections as their indicator of effectiveness. Imagine an organization whose personnel have bought into the notion that their reputations depend on doing well on an annual high-stakes inspection. Now add to the mix a reduction in personnel due to a drawdown and a concomitant loss of experienced leaders as well as an increase in workload. Something has to give, but lowering the standards is culturally viewed as unacceptable. Eventually the service members begin to recognize that they are playing a game that they cannot win, so they cheat—not because they are bad people, but because they desperately want to please their leaders and want their unit to look good in comparison with others.

There are various euphemisms for annotating records with work that was not actually completed, including "pencil whipping" or "gun decking." Sometimes the consequences can be staggering, as in the detainee abuse at Abu Ghraib Central Prison or the cheating scandal at Malmstrom Air Force Base. In the Malmstrom case, an investigation into drugs on the base uncovered that launch officers who were responsible for intercontinental nuclear missiles had been cheating on a monthly proficiency examination. Others in their unit knew that test answers were being shared, but they did not report the violation.[17] In that case, a statement by the commander of the Air Force's Global Strike Command was instructive:

> "Leadership's focus on perfection led commanders to micromanage their people," said Wilson, pointing to pressure to get 100% scores on monthly proficiency exams when only 90% was necessary to pass. ". . . Leaders lost sight of the fact that execution in the field is more important than what happens in the classroom."[18]

One-fifth of the intercontinental ballistic missile officers were decertified and taken off watch duty; ninety-two officers were connected to the cheating investigation.[19] When the force of approximately five hundred officers was retested, about 95 percent passed the test, indicating that most did not need to cheat to achieve an acceptable score.

Military leaders perceive that they are responsible for everything their unit does or fails to do. That notion drives a useful sense of accountability and serves as an antidote to inattentive or absentee leadership. It is a military maxim that tasks can be delegated but responsibility remains with the commander. Some leaders therefore feel that tasks will be accomplished only if they personally verify that work is accomplished to high standards. This attitude can be a recipe for both a helpful attention to detail and an unhelpful level of micromanagement where everything is a crisis and little is accomplished as a matter of routine. Conscientious leaders can become enmeshed in details better accomplished by those at lower levels, thereby elevating stress and undermining the authority of subordinate leaders. For example, at one military installation, a two-star general would frequently accost residents of family housing units because he felt their lawns needed mowing. During alerts, one battalion commander could be found checking the air pressure in the tires of military vehicles as they left the motor pool. Leaders are entitled to selectively dive deep into the inner workings of their organizations, but it does leave one to wonder how they have time to do their own work when they are attempting to do the jobs of others. Micromanagement serves as a "mechanism for staying in control and feeling powerful at the expense of others . . . Micromanaging and protecting one's territory are about guarding one's ego and absolute belief in being right above and beyond all others."[20]

Military organizations often foster a culture of "busyness." Military personnel can only accrue 90 days of annual leave, and any more than that is simply dropped from their leave and earnings statement at the end of the calendar year. In some units a leader's value to the organization is measured by the amount of annual leave that he or she loses at the end of the year. Some units have had to resort to draconian measures to ensure that military leaders actually take their authorized leave. Recognizing the importance of taking leave as a wellness issue, the commanding general of one unit told officers that if any of their subordinates lost annual leave they would have to report to him with an explanation as to why that service member was so important that they could not be allowed their authorized days off. In another instance, commanders were threatened with removal if they were found in their unit areas working past noon during the Christmas holiday period. The military workday begins early and runs late. At one hard-charging installation the commanding general threatened serious repercussions if commanders initiated physical training before 6 a.m. That leaves open to question how early commanders would otherwise stand formations if not for that directive. An old Army commercial bragged, "We do more before 9 a.m. than most people do all day." One officer joked that he was only working a half-day schedule—twelve hours equaled half a day. An old joke points out that if you take two naval surface warfare officers and put them in a room with nothing to do, they will soon be working twelve-hour shifts.

A strong work ethic is commendable, but workaholism can result in unnecessary exhaustion that leads to poor decisions, irritability, and loss of self-control. Military leaders rarely work in isolation. If the boss is working, conscientious subordinates are also likely to be on the job. Some semblance of work-life balance is necessary, not only for physical and mental well-being but also for the maintenance of healthy marital and family relationships.

The notion of chain of command is almost sacrosanct in military organizations, and the clear expression of supraordination and subordination is ingrained early in the socialization process. Subordinates are expected to bring their concerns first to their immediate supervisor, which helps to ensure that problems are corrected at the lowest possible level. Service members skip the chain of command at their peril as it is likely to garner negative reactions: from the higher-level supervisor who is faced with an issue that could have been solved at a lower level, and from the immediate supervisor who was skipped and now appears ineffective to their superiors. Although it is good that service members know exactly to whom they report and from whom they receive direction, adherence to the chain of command can also serve as a barrier to communication, distancing leaders from lower levels in the organization. It also places military personnel in a conundrum when their immediate supervisor is the problem. Most military organizations have mechanisms for accessing trusted agents outside the chain of command, including chaplains, mental health counselors, and the inspector general, but culture runs deep—there can be a reticence to make use of such services if it is perceived as a violation of the chain of command principle. Commanders are encouraged to establish an open door policy that permits any subordinate with an issue to seek an audience, but unit members are also encouraged to use the chain of command before involving the commander.

Military organizations tend to value loyalty, a complex and nuanced concept. At the most basic level, loyalty manifests as unflagging support of others at the unit level—loyalty to one's battle buddy, shipmate, crew, or fellow soldiers and immediate supervisors. Loyalty conflicts are relatively common, and unraveling them can require a sophisticated level of understanding. An example might serve to illustrate the point. Near a military installation a young woman was sexually assaulted, and the prime suspect was an army ranger. Key to the case was the location of the suspect, who claimed that he was in his barracks room at the time of the offense. Attention turned to the suspect's roommate, who was asked a simple question: "Was your roommate in the barracks at the time of the offense or not?" The young soldier refused to answer the question out of a sense of personal loyalty. No amount of cajoling or threatening would convince him to talk about his roommate's whereabouts. He was even threatened with obstruction of justice, a serious criminal offense. It was not until his regimental commander patiently explained the hierarchy of loyalty and the necessity of remaining loyal to principles beyond personal loyalty that the soldier provided the information and rebutted the alibi, and even then the information was given with a great sense of reticence and remorse.

A similar misplaced sense of loyalty to toxic supervisors can prevent their identification to those who have the power and authority to take action. Toxic leaders often play the loyalty card as a means of dissuading subordinates from making a complaint or raising concerns higher in the chain of command. Consider how whistle-blowers are frequently treated in military organizations. Despite the fact that they do the organization a great service by pointing out misconduct, their peers rarely appreciate their efforts. They might have done the right thing, but they can be perceived as disloyal for taking their observations to outsiders. Sometimes whistle-blowers require protection from retribution from other unit members, as was the case of Specialist Joe Darby who reported the detainee abuse at Abu Ghraib. Because he feared violence at the hands his fellow soldiers, special measures were put in place to ensure his safety.

The military fosters the notion that everyone is a leader, and just about everyone in the military will rise to leadership positions if he or she stays in the service long enough. There are no career privates; the military has an up or out personnel system, and all personnel in uniform are preparing for either their next level of responsibility or an exit from the armed services. Officers are rotated through command positions where their mettle is tested and their potential for higher-level command is assessed. Command, not a staff position, is considered the pathway to success. However, the sad truth is that not everyone who is slated for a leadership position is good at balancing task- and relationship-oriented behaviors in a way that is characteristic of good leadership. Everyone might get a chance to lead, but unfortunately not everyone will be good at it. Some would prefer to avoid command altogether, were it not for the negative impact that refusing it would have on their career trajectory.

## The Role of Followers

Susceptible followers serve an important function in perpetuating toxic leadership,[21] a topic that Jean Lipman-Blumen explored in detail in her book *The Allure of Toxic Leaders*.[22] "They commonly adulate, abet, and actually prefer toxic leaders to their nontoxic counterparts."[23] Our search for all-knowing, heroic leadership can blind us to the shortcomings of bad leaders and their impact. At the heart of it is an ingrained need for authority figures that is learned and reinforced from infancy. We may be predisposed to follow authority figures merely because they are authority figures.[24] We would rather have bad leadership than no leadership at all.

Toxic leaders often engage in a divide and conquer strategy that inculcates a feeling of helplessness in subordinates. In some cases, controlling supervisors parse information so only they see the entire picture. In other cases, they treat some members of the organization kindly while heaping abuse on others. On seeing the pain and suffering of the unfortunate targets, those who are spared are simply grateful that they are not in the crosshairs. They might be uncomfortable with the abusive treatment they witness, but they aren't inclined to be supportive of the downtrodden lest they incur the wrath of the boss as well. Those who are spared often make statements such as "He sure could be mean, but at least he wasn't mean to me." Sometimes they attribute their good fortune to their own superior performance: "She was abusive all right, but only with those who did not perform. She never had a problem with me."

When individuals feel powerless, there is a tendency to surrender to seemingly all-powerful leaders and to resort to coping behaviors or seeking an exit rather than taking the risk of challenging the leader or changing the dynamic.[25] When subordinates rally to each other for support and realize they all have options in dealing with a toxic leader, they become a threat. Thus, toxic leaders seek to implement mechanisms to fragment subordinates' power through excessive competition, passing divisive rumors, or creating in and out groups through the calculated use of rewards and coercion. Our prevailing culture and traditional leadership models encourage approaches that attempt to minimize or eliminate uncertainty. "Employees and the organization both avoid uncertainty. Employees want few surprises and they rarely get them"[26] Followers seek certainty and therefore tend to privilege leaders who provide a false but comforting sense of control and confidence. Much of it is an act or the product of self-delusion, but it beats the sense of helplessness that comes from admitting that a great deal is simply beyond our understanding and control. Even a toxic leader is preferable to surrendering to the undeterminable forces of chance. Wise leaders will engage in the hard work of increasing their subordinates' capacity to tolerate uncertainty, rather than manufacturing a false sense of certainty.[27]

Toxic leaders not only offer false certainty, they also create grand illusions through the articulation of noble visions—grandiose dreams that can be achieved if only subordinates obey the leader.[28] Our desire for a sense of meaning and purpose serves as a point of manipulation for the toxic leader. When seduced by a charismatic leader, susceptible followers can fall prey to "moral inversions" where bad becomes good.[29] In a classic example, "Gestapo leader Heinrich Himmler commended the members of the SS for their part in exterminating millions of people, an act that Himmler saw as 'a glorious page' in German history."[30] Striving to be the best unit and endeavoring to accomplish a seemingly important mission are not necessarily inappropriate or evil, but the intense drive to achieve such goals can serve to justify a multitude of sins. Visionary leaders become dangerous when their behaviors become exaggerated, disconnected from reality or self-centered, a phenomenon described as leadership's "dark side."[31] Charismatic toxic leaders tend to centralize power and in the process weaken authority structures that are normally dispersed throughout the organization.[32] That does not serve the organization well from a leader development point of view, and it leaves a power vacuum when the leader eventually departs.

Toxic leaders prefer compliant followers, but cowed and timid followers do not serve their organizations well. We should not be quick to let followers off the hook for the actions of supervisors. "We are responsible. Whether we lead or follow, we are responsible for the actions of those whom we can influence."[33] It is tempting to accept the role of helpless victim when suffering under a toxic leader as it absolves the follower of responsibility for the system of which they are an integral part. However, few in reality are totally helpless. Followers do have options although those options might involve risk or assuredly provoke painful outcomes that are not in their self-interest. There is a reason Ira Chaleff's book on the subject is entitled *The Courageous Follower*. There is little virtue in sycophantic, sheeplike followers. It takes courage to look powerful leaders in the eye and tell them what they need to hear rather than what they want to hear. It isn't always career enhancing, but it is sometimes the right thing to do.

Sometimes those who work for a toxic leader can serve the organization well by doing their best to mitigate the negative downstream impact. It is an emotionally exhausting and largely unappreciated role, but there has to be a special place in heaven for those who ably serve as a buffer between a toxic leader and lower-level subordinates. For example, a notoriously toxic senior leader called two of his subordinates into his office, who had had little to do with the event that triggered his anger but served as convenient outlets. He subjected them to an extensive tirade liberally laced with profanity and aspersions on their lineage and character, and when he was finally spent, he summarily dismissed them. As they left the room, but still within earshot of their volatile boss, the senior of the two showed extraordinary grace under pressure: he turned to the other and said, with characteristically good humor, "Gee, I thought that went well, didn't you?" Even the toxic leader was heard chuckling over that one. One executive officer took great pains to keep others up to date on the concerns, moods, and location of her toxic boss. She was quick to call subordinate leaders so they had time to prepare for an impending onslaught. She did so at personal risk, knowing that the toxic leader would likely see her actions as disloyal and react negatively. Those who received her heads-up calls were deeply appreciative of her efforts and considered her the ultimate team player.

Circumspection is advisable when considering the extent to which a subordinate can influence a truly toxic leader. Toxic leaders are notorious for rejecting negative feedback, especially from those who are lower in the organizational hierarchy.[34] Leading up is not for the faint of heart. Subordinates are not completely powerless, and they do have the ability to make a bad situation worse or better, but they do not have primary responsibility for fixing a bad boss. In military organizations the power differential is usually just too great for that to work. That job is in the purview of the boss's boss. Subordinates can be most effective in influencing toxic leaders indirectly, by understanding their boss's fears and concerns, and by ameliorating them as much as possible while facilitating the attainment of their goals. Good followers do what they can to encourage their supervisors to discover their better nature.

### Why Are They Toxic?

Determining the causes of toxic leadership rests in the domains of psychology and psychiatry, fields of expertise beyond the scope of this book, but it does not take a mental health professional to discern that at the heart of a great deal of toxic behavior lies a deep-seated sense of insecurity. Toxic leaders sometimes use aggressive and demeaning tactics to maintain emotional distance for fear that others might see through their façade and discover their inherent fragility and weakness. The Imposter Phenomenon refers to those who appear to be successful to others, but they have not internalized their success. Imposters fear being discovered by others when they cannot live up to high expectations.[35] High expectations are an inherent part of military leadership, especially under conditions of high demand that bring great stress. Imposters do not necessarily think more highly of themselves than others, and frequently they have an overall lack of positive self-regard.[36]

Toxic leaders experience feelings of inadequacy and feel better about themselves when putting others down. Insecurity, fear, and ambition can be a toxic combination. These leaders are frequently jealous of talented subordinates and can feel threatened by them. For instance, an especially talented company grade officer was nearing the end of a successful and demanding command tour. He graduated from the United States Military Academy at West Point, led his company in combat operations, and was widely known for his competence and martial abilities. He had recently been selected for a prestigious Olmstead scholarship. In one of his final days in the unit, as he passed his supervisor, a lieutenant colonel, the boss noticed a small hole in the captain's tee-shirt where the collar had begun to separate from the underlying fabric. His boss moved very close to the officer, put his finger in the hole to hook the collar, and tore a gaping hole in the tee-shirt before menacingly ordering the captain to return when he was in proper uniform. It was a power play pure and simple, and one designed to put the young captain firmly in his place, as if to say, "You're not so much." The captain literally shook with rage but maintained his composure and bearing. Such behavior brings to mind the character of Daniel Plainview in the feature-length film *There Will Be Blood*, played by Daniel Day Lewis, who said, "I have a competition in me. I want no one else to succeed. I hate most people."[37]

Toxic followers are easier to deal with once identified, and by understanding that insecurity is a key driver of toxic leadership behavior, subordinates can endeavor to make their supervisors feel more secure. They can try to avoid behavior that will feed the paranoia that is often lurking near the surface by being supportive so long as the organization's goals and objectives are not compromised in the process. Toxic leaders are anxious to be offended and are easily slighted, so care should be taken to avoid embarrassing them, especially in public. The toxic leader might be motivated primarily by self-interest, but that isn't necessarily a problem if those interests coincide with the interests of the organization. Followers can focus on performing their duties well and taking pride in their accomplishments, understanding that competence is not an insurance policy against outbursts from a toxic leader. Not every criticism from an overly critical boss should to be taken to heart. Internalizing the constant complaining and unrelenting negativity of a toxic leader is a losing game—a ticket to ulcers, depression, or worse.

Focus lands on toxic leaders because of their wide wake of destruction. A bad sergeant is a problem, but a bad general is a catastrophe. Senior officers cast a much broader swath of influence. Outside of leadership roles, toxic followers do exist, and they can wreak havoc in organizations by disrupting colleagues, undermining leaders, and poisoning unit climate. They thrive when their supervisors are inattentive or unwilling to intervene. In an effort to keep the peace, colleagues can easily become complicit in the behavior of toxic peers as well. In an effort to minimize conflict, colleagues will avoid them or tacitly enable their destructive influence. As British philosopher John Stuart Mill once said, "Bad men need nothing more to compass their ends, than that good men should look on and do nothing."[38]

# 4   The Role of Narcissism in Toxic Leadership

> When the healthy pursuit of self-interest and self-realization
> turns into self-absorption, other people can lose their intrinsic
> value in our eyes and become mere means to the fulfillment
> of our needs and desires.
>
> —P. M. Forni

An ancient Greek myth tells the story of Narcissus, who was
adored by many yet loved no others in return. He enjoyed the
attention that was lavished upon him as a result of his physique,
but he had no equal in beauty and therefore felt others were
unworthy of him. Various versions of the story exist, but they
typically involve him spurning the heartfelt advances of another.
In retribution for his arrogance the gods punished him by leading
him to his image reflected in a pool of water. Not realizing it was
his own reflection, he became thoroughly enamored. When he
realized that his love could not be returned, one version holds that
he killed himself; another version has him wasting away, unable
to tear himself away from his reflection. The term *narcissism* has
come to describe those who hold themselves in excessive esteem
or those who are exceptionally self-absorbed. Self-aggrandizing
behavior has an amplifying effect in toxic leadership, and those

with an inflated sense of self-worth have a propensity to engage in problematic interpersonal behavior as well as flawed decision making that contributes to the perception of their leadership as toxic. The characteristics of narcissism are therefore worthy of additional examination.

Grandiose belief systems and narcissistic styles are frequently associated with the rise and fall of notorious and infamous leaders such as Adolph Hitler, Joseph Stalin, and Saddam Hussein, but what connects them most is their egotistical need for power and disregard for those they lead.[1] Arrogance and self-aggrandizement are not virtues, and those who must constantly prove their superiority to themselves and others can be difficult to live with. When their grandiosity drives them to overreach, they can lead themselves, their constituents, and their organizations to ruin through the application of charm or intimidation.

Older people often complain that the younger generation is going to hell in a handbasket, a phenomenon that was as just as true with our great grandparents as it is today. However, there is some evidence that narcissism levels are indeed on the rise. The level of narcissism in American college students as measured by the Narcissistic Personality Inventory increased significantly between 1979 and 2006. Almost two-thirds of college students in 2006 were above the mean narcissism score of 1979 to 1985, reflecting an increase of 30 percent.[2] Because narcissists seek attention and self-serving ends without concern for the impact they have on others, an increase in the prevalence of narcissism could suggest a corresponding rise in toxic leadership. Care should be taken, however, when making such generalizations because broad, sweeping statements seldom capture the variety found within generations.

### An Unholy Trio: Bullying, Cronyism, and Narcissism

Ronald E. Riggio, the Henry R. Kravis Professor of Leadership and Organizational Psychology at Claremont McKenna College, considers bullying, cronyism, and narcissism an "unholy trio" that contributes to workplace toxicity.[3] In his *Psychology Today* article on the subject, he wrote, "All too often, these bullies feel justified for their actions against victims. Since they can do no wrong (in their own minds), the victim is the problem, and the bullies feel justified in their persecution. My guess is the intent is to bully the person in order to get the victim to quit. The misguided bullies believe, in their narcissistic thinking, that this will create a better workplace."[4] For example, one particularly ruthless toxic general regarded subordinate evaluations as his chance to "cull the herd." If he wasn't terminating someone's career, he felt he just wasn't doing his job. He had no compunctions about comparing his followers to cattle, and his evaluations frequently matched his callous opinions.

People with narcissistic tendencies are likely to misattribute good outcomes to their own behavior and bad outcomes to insufficient skills or poor efforts of others. Others are never as worthy or as smart as the narcissist, so when things do not go as planned, it is always someone else's fault. Accordingly the documentary that charted the rise and meteoric fall of Enron, the notorious energy trading company, was called *Enron: The Smartest Guys in the Room*.[5] The Enron story has become a symbol of destructive leadership stemming from a toxic corporate culture. Enron was a successful and innovative Texas-based energy trading company with over 63 billion dollars in assets. By the end of 2001 the share price was less than one dollar, and the company was filing for bankruptcy. That failure also led to the dissolution of Enron's auditor, Arthur Andersen, and widespread changes in the accounting industry. Some executives at Enron, such as CEO Jeffrey Skilling, engaged in unethical practices including the use of shady accounting practices to over report profits and fratboy, testosterone-fueled behavior in the CEO suite. For example, according to the Enron documentary, Lou Pai, the head of Enron's Energy Services subsidiary, was motivated by two things: money and strippers, whom he allegedly sometimes charged to corporate accounts. Skilling enjoyed risk and organized adventurous, sometimes dangerous trips for friends and customers. He also suffered from delusions of grandeur: at one point he was heard to proclaim, "I am Enron." Emboldened by a moribund board of directors and inattentive regulators, Enron's leaders believed that so long as they were making money for their investors in the short term little else mattered. Although the debacle had many contributing factors, it is not hard to see the role of arrogant narcissistic leadership at the center of what was then the world's largest bankruptcy.

As with Narcissus, an excessive focus on self as the center of everything good can contribute to a lack of empathy and compassion for others, a behavior that is characteristic of toxic leadership. There is nothing wrong with a healthy level of ambition, and some degree of self-interest is a necessary ingredient for helpful notions like pride and honor. Also, if there is no element of self-respect, the drive to be held in high regard by others which promotes some very helpful behaviors is also missing. The organization benefits when the best and brightest aspire and strive to achieve leadership positions, but those who cannot discern the difference between their own interests and those of the organization can become relentless career climbers who will do just about anything to advance their interests. They rationalize their self-centered behavior and see themselves as exceptional in the sense that rules that apply to others do not apply to them. They become immune to the suffering of others if their own interests are being furthered, and because they believe themselves to be smarter than others, they tend to stop listening or become overly critical. They tend to feel entitled to privileges not afforded to others because they deserve them as a result of the unique and indispensable service they are providing to their organizations.

Good leaders understand that leadership is a team sport that requires a "we" and not a "me" mentality. Generations of military officers have benefited from the literary contribution of Anton Myer, who provided a vivid description of two fundamental types of leaders in his classic novel *Once an Eagle*.[6] The character Sam Damon represented the sincere and selfless officer who progressed by virtue of his competence. For him every promotion was merely a means to additional service, almost a byproduct of his good performance. Courtney Massingale provided the counterexample: a clever career climber and organizational chameleon who was ever focused on the next promotion and used relationships as a tool for his own advancement. Individuals fitting both the Sam Damon and Courtney Massingale archetypes can be easily identified in today's military.

Narcissists are frequently found in positions of power and responsibility because they tend to self-nominate for challenging leadership positions. They might not be the best at leading others, but they seek the limelight that leadership roles provide, eclipsing those who might be more capable but are also more humble and selfless—and correspondingly less visible. Narcissists want and need the power that comes with leadership positions to implement their grandiose visions of the future. Their skillful use of relationships places them in the orbit of influential people for whom they make themselves indispensable, and their self-promoting behaviors bring them to the attention of powerful people who make decisions about key assignments and positions. The confidence and sense of certainty they bring to such roles is often appreciated, at least for a while. The polish leaves the apple only after their manipulative and unethical behaviors come to light and their counterproductive impact becomes obvious. In the military, such leaders often are promoted or have moved to their next set of victims before their impact becomes apparent.

As with other concepts in this book the question is not whether a person is narcissistic but the extent to which a person is narcissistic and whether that leads to helpful or dysfunctional leadership behavior. We are all narcissistic to some degree. Some amount of self-promotion is beneficial and necessary in order to be noticed in a competitive and bureaucratic system, but an excessive amount is no virtue. As with most aspects of personality there is a curvilinear relationship with narcissism and effectiveness. Some narcissism translates to a confident outgoing personality, but as the level of narcissism increases so too does the propensity for abuse of power and unethical behavior.[7] Self-confidence is an essential element for those who would take on leadership roles and positional responsibilities, but "frequently wrong yet never in doubt" is not a recipe for success.

## Narcissistic Personality Disorder

The American Psychiatric Association recognizes narcissism as a diagnosable personality disorder if five or more of the following criteria are manifested in an ingrained and enduring pattern that is inflexible across a range of personal and professional situations.

- Has a grandiose sense of self-importance (e.g., exaggerates achievements and talents, expects to be recognized as superior without commensurate achievements).
- Is preoccupied with fantasies of unlimited success, power, brilliance, beauty, or ideal love.
- Believes that he or she is "special" and unique and can only be understood by, or should associate with, other special or high-status people (or institutions).
- Requires excessive admiration.
- Has a sense of entitlement—unreasonable expectations of especially favorable treatment or automatic compliance with his or her expectations.
- Is interpersonally exploitative—takes advantage of others to achieve his or her own ends.
- Lacks empathy—is unwilling to recognize or identify with the feelings and needs of others.
- Is often envious of others or believes that others are envious of him or her.
- Shows arrogant, haughty behaviors or attitudes.[8]

Narcissistic behavior is not always problematic nor does it necessarily call for a mental health intervention. To qualify for a psychiatric diagnosis the narcissistic behavior must lead to significant distress or impairment in functioning. Some narcissistic behavior can be beneficial. Military notables who could be described as narcissistic include Napoleon Bonaparte and Alexander the Great, to name but two. Michael Maccoby has noted there is a difference between productive and unproductive narcissists.[9] Productive narcissists are visionary, audacious risk takers who passionately pursue their dreams and thrive in periods of chaos. George S. Patton Jr. and Douglas MacArthur might fit the description of productive narcissists. Unproductive narcissists are typically emotionally isolated and distrustful. An important characteristic for the exploration of toxic leadership rests with this observation: unproductive narcissists tend to react with rage when confronted with what they perceive as threats. As a result they do not deal well with dissent, preferring agreement to an airing of various points of view. Such people indoctrinate rather than teach, dominate meetings, are convinced of their superior abilities, are sensitive to criticism, want to be understood but lack empathy for others, find it difficult to mentor or be mentored, and are relentless and ruthless competitors.[10]

Narcissistic leaders are problematic largely because of the impact their behavior has on interpersonal relationships. They are more likely to foster resentment than trust and confidence, even if they are otherwise intelligent and competent. They are loath to admit a mistake, so their subordinates become scapegoats for things that go wrong. Their search for a scapegoat leads to their attributing psychological pathologies to others. Their callous disregard of others, emotional distance, and tendency to exploit relationships for personal gain trigger negative, unproductive reactions in their followers, yet the narcissists are often surprised to discover that others feel or react in these ways. When confronted with the negative implications of their behavior, narcissists feel profoundly misunderstood, and they are quick to perceive their followers as disloyal and their supervisors as mistaken. Some are quick to be offended, and their hypersensitivity to threats or insults makes them volatile. Quick to find humor in the foibles of others, they are notoriously unable to take a joke when it is directed at them. Resentment on the part of their followers may erupt, but it is more likely to simmer for long periods of time because followers quickly learn that direct confrontation is a dangerous path.

## Narcissism and Pathologies of Decision Making

Narcissism can also negatively impact the decision-making process, an issue that should be of particular concern to military organizations. Although much may be said for the lone genius, collective judgments are often more consistently accurate, especially when they are the product of robust dialogue and contest rather than compliance alone.[11] Because of their feelings of superiority, narcissistic supervisors are not as likely to encourage the frank and honest exchange of information that results in better decision-making processes. They tend to be more appreciative of sycophants who bolster their ego and never risk overshadowing or disagreeing with the boss. Because of their deep-seated need to maintain a façade of invulnerability, these leaders can be dismissive of information that counters their delusions or threatens their public image. They rarely admit mistakes, are slow to access the ideas of subordinates, and are quick to blame others for things that go wrong. Some toxic narcissists are vigilant for opportunities to humble others, especially subordinates who show potential or may be perceived as stealing the limelight.

As contemporary operating environments become more volatile, uncertain, complex, and ambiguous, the cognitive abilities of a lone person are increasingly likely to fall short. Narcissists are not comfortable in environments that call for harnessing the collective capacity of others; they will seek to control the agenda to limit open dialogue, or restrict the membership of deliberative groups to those they perceive as agreeing with them. Self-censorship and a sole focus on pleasing a supervisor become a problem when they lead to poor decisions. Subordinates may begin to prefer organizational failure rather than face a tantrum from their supervisor, and they may choose to remain silent despite seeing likely negative outcomes. At worst, they become so antagonized that they are willing to accept or facilitate organizational failure if it will make their boss look bad.

In an environment where subordinates do not feel comfortable airing their opinions, it is unlikely that a group will explore a full range of alternatives. Getting the right answer becomes less important than giving the boss what he or she wants to hear. Narcissists are unlikely to delegate tasks or empower others because of a belief that followers will not perform to an acceptable standard. In this case "acceptable standard" is code for not how the boss would do it. As a result subordinates are denied opportunities for growth and development while the narcissist becomes increasingly busy and overwhelmed. When they do engage in independent decision making, subordinates are frequently subjected to a stream of criticism that erodes their confidence. They become less motivated to engage in preemptive or innovative behavior, defaulting to merely executing their supervisor's instructions. In a descending spiral of effectiveness, supervisors then become frustrated that their subordinates lack initiative and loose another torrent of confidence-eroding criticism. In organizations where the only good idea is the boss's idea, good followers often find ways carefully to lead their supervisor to a right decision and convince the supervisor that it was his or her idea all along. Such self-effacing behavior may be effective with narcissists, but it is also exhausting and thankless work.

Dartmouth professor of management Sydney Finkelstein explored massive corporate failures in *Why Smart Executives Fail* and identified patterns of executive leadership behavior that have contributed to organizational declines of catastrophic proportions. Finkelstein's chapter on "Seven Habits of Spectacularly Unsuccessful People" contains a useful litany of bad leadership practices that have preceded collapses.[12] Many contributing factors to failure originated from the top levels of the organizations. Some executives exhibited toxic tendencies, but most of the dysfunctional behaviors stemmed from, or were exacerbated by, narcissistic tendencies. Although Finkenstein and his team studied failure in the corporate sector, many of the bad habits they identified are equally if not more applicable in the national security and military settings.

*Habit 1:* Unsuccessful executives see themselves and their companies as dominating their environments, not simply responding to developments in those environments. Narcissists might be particularly prone to this fatal habit. The mantra "We're number one" is stimulating, and everyone enjoys being on a winning team, but there is no more effective narcotic to deaden creativity, innovation, and change than the perception that you are on top and cannot lose. Between World War I and World War II the Germans engaged in extensive change that led to advances in maneuver warfare that almost conquered the world. The French, who had won World War I, had little motivation to change, leading to continued investment in existing yet increasingly outmoded tactics and structures. This mindset was epitomized by their extensive fortifications along the Maginot Line, which proved ineffective when the German army maneuvered around them. The German army also effectively implemented air-ground operations and exploitive maneuvers using tanks and other mechanized formations that were coordinated through widespread use of radio communications. These approaches were not unknown to the French, they hadn't capitalized on the ideas. Freed of investment in costly legacy systems, the Germans innovated for a new war while the French continued to fight the last one.

Organizations with stagnant habits are prone to strategic surprises when they underestimate their competitors or adversaries. Some corporate leaders find themselves the beneficiaries of great wealth and success as the result of an uptick in the business cycle, but they convince themselves that it was actually a result of their talent and ingenuity. Likewise, some in the military come to believe inflated narratives in their fitness and evaluation reports, reinforcing their sense of self-esteem and delusions of infallibility. Underestimating the enemy has been the bane of many a battlefield commander. In one of the most famous instances of underestimation, Lieutenant Colonel George Armstrong Custer seemed more concerned that 1,500 to 2,000 Lakota, Cheyenne, and Arapahoe warriors at the Battle of Little Bighorn might break into smaller groups and escape than present a legitimate threat to his forces. "He was flamboyant and ambitious. He was habitually aggressive and reckless. He was fearless in battle. He was notorious for stretching his superiors' orders, taking risks and, through skill and 'Custer's Luck,' succeeding against improbable odds."[13] A great deal of myth surrounds "Custer's last stand," but it is now generally accepted that in less than two hours after the commencement of the attack Custer and most of his men were killed.[14]

*Habit 2:* Unsuccessful executives identify so completely with the company that there is no clear boundary between their personal interests and corporate interests. Because of their propensity to view their own interests as the central frame of reference, leaders with narcissistic tendencies may be particularly susceptible to this bad habit. Those who serve in the public sector are expected to put the public interest ahead of their own, and they should certainly take care to avoid conflicts of interest or use of public resources for themselves. Misappropriation of public funds or resources and misuse of subordinates for personal services are two mistakes that can stem from blurred boundaries. Military aircraft may be designated for use by some officials when they are on official business, but officials who conflate their personal needs with the public interest are misusing such assets. For example, a secretary of the army was accused of flying a military plane to the sale of his 6.5 million dollar vacation home.[15] A marine brigadier general was formally reprimanded for ordering a C-12 Beechcraft to shuttle him between the El Toro Marine Corps Air Station and the marines' Big Bear Lake Recreational Facility in California during a trip with his fiancée. The general's conduct drew particular scrutiny because he had previously dismissed two of his top aides over allegations that they had used aircraft for golfing jaunts and other personal business; one of the aides committed suicide a few days after his suspension.[16]

Excessive personal identification is also problematic if it results in an inability to acknowledge a bad decision. For some, the admission of a bad decision equates to an admission that they are not a good leader; to avoid this indictment they will escalate their commitment to their bad ideas. In other words, their inability to admit a mistake causes them to expend unnecessary resources in nonproductive areas, a flaw that can have catastrophic consequences on the battlefield.

*Habit 3:* Unsuccessful executives seem to have all the answers, often dazzling people with the speed and decisiveness with which they can deal with challenging issues. Their success in being promoted to positions of responsibility reinforces their approach and ways of thinking. They are often extraordinarily successful in many aspects of their lives to the extent that they come to believe even more in their own infallibility. Decisiveness is a good thing, but only if the decisions are correct. There is little virtue in ignoring information that suggests a preferred course of action is a bad idea. Finkelstein used the example of Samsung Motors to illustrate a case where neither tenacity nor determination could stand in the face of a fundamentally bad idea. The Korean manufacturing conglomerate Samsung had a very successful history in producing consumer electronics and appliances. Despite plentiful evidence indicating that a foray into the automobile market would be ill advised—a significant drop in demand for cars and consolidation in the Korean car market—the previously outrageously successful executive team launched an ambitious and ultimately unsuccessful car company. It had not been a good idea at day one, and it was still a bad idea 5 billion dollars later. Eventually Samsung had to sell ten of its companies and reduce its labor force by 50,000 to survive.[17]

Narcissists have a tendency to ignore or dismiss information that is inconsistent with their self-centered worldview. After all, those who know it all have little reason to listen to or value the opinions of others. A military example of Habit 3 might be found in the stubborn insistence of some World War I generals on using Napoleonic tactics in the face of modern weapon systems, including automatic weapons. The Battle of the Somme in northern France was a characteristic example of these epic exercises in futility. On the morning of July 1, 1916, Field Marshal Sir Douglas Haig, chief of staff of the British Expeditionary Force, ordered 110,000 soldiers to attack from their trenches. Within a few hours they had experienced 60,000 casualties, and almost 20,000 were killed without gaining a single objective. Haig would persist in such attacks for another four months.

*Habit 4:* Unsuccessful executives make sure that everyone is 100 percent behind them, ruthlessly eliminating anyone who might undermine their efforts. In every case of massive organizational failure there were good-hearted, dedicated, and loyal members who tried to point out the downsides of a bad course of action, and they were summarily fired or relegated to some form of organizational Siberia. In one police organization members clearly knew who was in favor or not based on their assignments: everyone knew that "permanent midnight shift commander" was the position for someone in trouble with the chief. Narcissists do not bear criticism well, even when couched in the form of loyal dissent. Their deep-seated insecurity triggers a rage response when they are confronted, especially when the confrontation could damage their image. Not everyone who disagrees is an enemy, yet that is how dissenters are frequently treated. Such intolerance of dissent diminishes the warning signals that could avert catastrophe. By eliminating those who will speak truth to power, the leader becomes increasingly surrounded by those who reinforce the boss's ego, who will avoid telling him or her necessary information. Sycophantic followers become the enablers who facilitate the organization's decline.

*Habit 5:* Unsuccessful executives are consummate company spokespersons, often devoting the largest portion of their efforts to managing and developing the company image. A focus on image and form over function is so ubiquitous in the military that it could almost be called characteristic. Keeping the troops busy through meaningless tasks such as painting rocks, searching for litter, excessively buffing floors, or similar tasks of minimal significance with an unrelenting focus on looking good rather than being good are characteristics of this bad habit. One senior military leader ordered his unit to fluff the snow banks outside of the headquarters because he felt dirty snow reflected poorly on the unit (and himself). Another would throw a fit if paperclips were not attached to documents in an exact way. A commander who was largely disengaged from daily operations of the unit would become engaged only during visits from superiors or important visitors, whereupon no detail was beneath his attention. Such habits lead to burnished reputations with outsiders, but underneath lies a shallow, ineffective leadership approach.

*Habit 6:* Unsuccessful executives underestimate major obstacles. "They become so enamored with their vision of what they want to achieve that they overlook the difficulty of actually getting there."[18] Nothing is hard for those who do not have to do the work. When prior success comes easy, narcissists begin to believe that they cannot fail, and their heightened sense of self-importance leads them to disregard the significance of inevitable hurdles. There is a military maxim that holds that tactics are for amateurs while professionals focus on logistics. History provides numerous examples of instances where military organizations were tactically sound yet faltered due to inattention to logistical details. The experience of the American military in the Spanish American War serves as an example. The American soldiers fought well and valiantly, but it was apparent that the nation was unprepared to mobilize, equip, and project a large force over long distances. Secretary of War Elihu Root was convinced that most of the mistakes of the war with Spain were the result of faulty planning and inadequate organization. As an example, when U.S. forces arrived in Cuba there were not enough boats to ferry troops and animals to the shore. Some men were dropped off too far from the shallows, so they were dragged down by the weight of their equipment and drowned. Horses also were unloaded haphazardly, resulting in the loss of a precious asset. One of the most famous participants of the landing in Cuba, Theodore Roosevelt, reported disembarking with rifles, ammunition belts, and not much else—the extent of his camp equipment for three days was the food in his pocket and a light coat. The armed forces would repeat many of the logistical mistakes associated with the over the shore operations experienced in the North African campaign in the later operations in Sicily and Italy during World War II. As Pulitzer prize winning author Rick Atkinson noted in *The Day of Battle: The War In Sicily and Italy, 1943–1945*,

> Seven different directives on how to label overseas cargo had been issued the previous year, the resulting confusion led to the formation of the inevitable committee, which led to another directive called the Schenectady Plan, which led to color-coded labels lacquered onto shipping containers, which led to more confusion. Five weeks after issuing a secret alert called Preparations for Movement by Water, the Army discovered that units critical to [Operation] HUSKY had never received the order and thus had no plans for loading their troops, vehicles, and weapons onto the convoys. Seventh Army's initial load plans also neglected to make room for the Army Air Forces, whose kit equaled a third of the Army's total tonnage requirements. Every unit pleaded for more space; every unit claimed priority; every unit lamented the Navy's insensitivity.[19]

Success in North Africa might have dulled the impetus to make changes that were needed before the next campaign. Drawing arrows on a map and commanding, "follow me" are apparently not the most complicated aspects of military operations.

*Habit 7:* Unsuccessful executives stubbornly rely on what worked for them in the past. Those who lack self-awareness are prone to revert to past approaches in dealing with problems, especially when under stress. Past performance is no guarantee of future success, especially when key factors in the environment or situation have changed. Unsuccessful executives often have significant strengths, and those strengths are rewarded and reinforced by the organization. Shadows come with the bright spots, however, and if not mitigated they can derail not only the executive but the organization as well. Narcissists can be quite effective in denying the negative aspects of their personality and placing the blame for their failings on others. During a large training exercise an officer insisted on personally reconnoitering the location where his higher headquarters was relocating. His immediate subordinate dutifully drove his boss to the site, cautioning that if they were to join the departing convoy they would have to return by a specified time. The superior casually examined the site and ignored several warnings that they were going to be late for the convoy. When they did return, sure enough, they had missed the movement, causing them to straggle in noticeably late. Embarrassed, the officer publicly berated his subordinate, furiously blaming him for the situation. Toxic narcissists can be slow to learn and adapt to changing conditions. They are often overconfident and do not learn from their mistakes.[20] Some will acknowledge the darker aspects of their leadership style, but are seemingly unwilling or unable to modify their approach.

In a recent *Military Review* article, Doty and Fenlason asserted that most, if not all, toxic leaders are also narcissistic.[21] While narcissistic and toxic leadership are different concepts, they are related, and what counts for one often applies to the other. The overlapping circles of a Venn diagram come to mind wherein two concepts overlap in significant but not all ways. Some behaviors that have a destructive impact on an organization, such as absenteeism or timidity, do not involve narcissism, but it is not hard to see how toxicity can stem from narcissistic behavior. The self-centered focus of narcissists makes them relatively unskilled at understanding, interpreting, and reacting to the emotions of others, which psychologists Mayer, Salovey, and Caruso attribute to their deficit in "emotional intelligence."[22]

In his book *Emotional Intelligence*, psychologist Daniel Goleman famously asserted that emotional intelligence sometimes matters more than IQ.[23] Those who are emotionally intelligent are good at reading, understanding, and empathizing with others. Some might equate emotional intelligence to "people skills," critical in building strong relationships with others. Business writer Chip Conley identified a list of emotionally intelligent chief executive officers that included Howard Schultz of Starbucks, who returned to the company out of love for the company and its people, and Alan Mulally of Ford Motor Company, who is known for great interpersonal skills and an ability to make people feel as though they are the only one in the room when he is speaking.[24] Although intelligence (IQ) still seems to explain a great deal of success in leadership roles, Goleman's assertion about the primacy of emotional intelligence is arguably valid: a lack of emotional intelligence would seem to account for those who are plenty smart yet also manifest disheartening interpersonal behavior.

Subordinates tend to appreciate supervisors who are emotionally intelligent and attuned to their needs. Emotional intelligence appears to contribute to effective performance and more committed employees because emotionally intelligent leaders demonstrate an understanding of what it takes to keep people working as a team.[25] They engage in developing others and in relationship-oriented behaviors that are correlated with positive perceptions of leadership. One study asserted that more than 55 percent of organizational climate can be attributable to the manager's level of emotional intelligence.[26]

### Surviving Narcissistic Leaders

Those who attempt to helpfully intervene with a person who has narcissistic tendencies are in for some heavy lifting. Working with and for narcissists can be a challenge, whether they merely have narcissistic tendencies or, in the worst-case scenario, have a narcissistic personality disorder. A diagnosis of narcissistic personality disorder indicates an extreme case, and long-term psychotherapy typically is the treatment. Although cognitive behavioral or group therapies can be beneficial, they generally rely on a patient admitting to having a problem, which does not fit with a narcissist's inflated sense of self; they are unlikely to seek help or appreciate it when it is offered. Toxic narcissists might not be so debilitated as to require treatment, but they can be expected to avoid seeking help and to react negatively to suggestions that they would benefit from some intervention. Military commanders and supervisors have a useful tool at their disposal: they can order subordinates to undergo a mental health evaluation.[27]

Rather than focusing on underlying causes and diagnoses, supervisors of those with narcissistic tendencies should focus on close monitoring, early identification of problematic behaviors, and clear, direct expression of what is acceptable and what is not. Those with narcissistic tendencies bear considerable watching, and supervisors should not hesitate to coach, advise, or redirect them when the dark side of their personality emerges.

Although it would be a mistake to blame victims for their oppression or hold them accountable for fixing toxic leaders, followers are part of the social system, and they do have some responsibility for the organizational dynamics that take place around them. Followers aren't necessarily responsible for the actions of their supervisors, but they are responsible for their own actions in reaction to narcissistic and toxic supervisors. A follower's actions can make things better—or far worse. Maccoby has supplied three useful tips to help those who work for a narcissist.[28]

*Tip 1:* Empathize with the boss's feelings but do not expect empathy in return. It is important to understand that behind the display of infallibility that narcissists project is a deep sense of vulnerability that motivates much of their behavior. A narcissist will see through flattery and prefer those who are truly appreciative of their talents. They need to know that their image will be protected, they will resent any feedback that threatens their inflated self-image, and they will likely retaliate when their delusions of grandeur are challenged. Those who need support and positive reinforcement from their supervisor are likely to be disappointed and unfulfilled when working for a narcissist. Those who seek and need approval from supervisors to bolster their self-image are not likely to get what they need from narcissists. Living in a constant stream of negativity can be exceedingly taxing, so those working for a narcissist should look for self-esteem elsewhere. Sometimes that may come from healthy associations with others like family, peers, or subordinates. Satisfaction can also be found in the completion of a job well done even when it is not often recognized as such from an immediate supervisor. Hobbies, sports, spiritual practices, or other nonwork activities can be sources of diversion and solace.

*Tip 2:* Give the boss good ideas but always let them take the credit. Their image is of primary importance, so they are likely to appreciate those who are useful in making them look good. A follower should find out what the boss thinks before presenting views and opinions. It is not necessary or advisable to blindly agree with everything the boss says or does, but the use of tact and interpersonal skill when dissenting are necessary elements for survival. Narcissists expect loyalty from below, but they are not necessarily inclined to be loyal to subordinates from above. Disagree when appropriate, but in the process demonstrate how the boss will benefit from a different point of view. The best way to disagree with a narcissist is to illustrate how a different course of action would be in their best interest.

*Tip 3:* Narcissistic leaders often assign subordinates more tasks than they can accomplish, so good time management skills are beneficial. It is a good idea to study the supervisor and learn to discern the difference between important tasks and those that are relatively unimportant. Maccoby makes the risky suggestion that because narcissists often forget about the directions they give their subordinates, followers should simply ignore those that do not make sense. When following that suggestion prudence is advisable: toxic narcissists are likely to react strongly if they perceive they are being ignored or if failure to complete a task later reflects negatively on their image. Be aware of the boss's schedule and be strategic about taking time off. It is usually best to take leave or vacation when there is a lull in his or her schedule. Some supervisors return from trips anxious and full of new ideas; others tend to bask in the glow of a successful excursion and for a brief period are easier to work with. Understanding and reacting accordingly to such patterns of behavior can make working for a narcissist a bit more tolerable.

# 5 Toxic Leadership and Sexual Misconduct

> Sexual assault is a shameful and disgusting crime. Failing to intervene if you witness it is a cowardly act.
>
> —Michael P. Barrett, Sergeant Major of the Marine Corps

If an individual in a group meets common expectations of its members and acts in ways that benefit the group, over a period of time they accumulate social credit and status. They obtain a reputation for good leadership and amass willing followers. A bank account serves as a suitable analogy. Every time a leader of an organization makes a good decision or is perceived as acting in the interests of the group, that leader is making a deposit in the bank of goodwill. That repository permits them to occasionally deviate from group expectations and norms to do things that are unusual or unexpected. If the deposits have been sufficient, followers will forgive the occasional deviation. Consider the leader who is usually right but uncharacteristically makes a bad call. Because of an earned reputation of good decision making, the leader's followers retain faith and confidence. However, if a leader overdraws the account through a series of unmet expectations or an overwhelming breach of faith, followers and other organizational stakeholders lose confidence and are likely to withdraw the supervisor's permission to lead. Hollander called this notion "idiosyncrasy credit."[1] Sexual misconduct is a behavior that is not only corrosive to good order and discipline in military organizations, it also constitutes an overwhelming breach of faith, especially when it involves subordinates. It constitutes a form of toxic leadership that has a decidedly negative impact on organizational climate.

## Impact of Sexual Misconduct

Leaders benefit from being perceived as composed and in control. Those who demonstrate an inability to restrain their sexual impulses become suspect in the eyes of followers. Unwanted sexual contact, especially between superiors and subordinates in the chain of command, qualifies as toxic because it meets the operational definition proffered in Chapter 1: an apparent lack of regard for the welfare of subordinates and an interpersonal style that degrades organizational climate. Supervisors might not be engaging in the behavior to get ahead in the career sense, but they are using a subordinate for their own selfish interests. Sometimes disputed allegations of sexual misconduct fracture the unit into groups that support either the victim or the alleged assailant. Unit social cohesion, esprit de corps, and unity of purpose are frequently degraded under such conditions.

Using a subordinate as an object for sexual gratification exemplifies a lack of regard that is characteristic of toxic leadership, and the deleterious impact of sexual misconduct, especially on the victim, can be catastrophic in nature. The impact of sexual assault is unlike other crimes in that it can leave deep-rooted physical and psychological effects on the victim with potentially lifelong consequences.[2]

There is a well-documented association between experiences of sexual assault and harassment during military service and poor health. Generally, studies have shown that men and women experience similar levels of psychological symptoms and distress after experiencing military sexual assault or harassment, with the most common mental health conditions for both being posttraumatic stress disorder, depression, anxiety disorders and substance abuse disorders.[3]

The impact of sexual misconduct spreads beyond the victim to include friends and family members and the organization as a whole. Even if the misconduct is consensual and does not rise to the level of assault, the impact on preexisting intimate relationships in the form of loss of trust and sense of betrayal are fairly obvious.

When speaking of sexual misconduct, improper relationships, harassment, sexual violence, and rape, some specificity is appropriate to prevent otherwise well-meaning people from talking past each other. It might be helpful to think of sexual misconduct on a scale, with consensual but prohibited sexual contact on one end and rape on the other. Unlawful romance between two adults is wrong and worthy of sanction under certain circumstances in military settings; sexual assault can involve brutal acts of violence that are unconscionable under any circumstances.

As this chapter was being written, the *Washington Post* reported that the army had just demoted a one-star general to the rank of lieutenant colonel and fined him 20,000 dollars for a three-year affair with a subordinate officer.[4] That case garnered headlines because of salacious allegations that he had sexually assaulted the subordinate but had pled guilty to lesser offenses of adultery, maltreatment of a subordinate, engaging in improper relations, and other charges. Unfortunately such high profile cases are not isolated incidents. The *Washington Post* reported thirty U.S. generals and admirals had been investigated for personal misconduct since October 2012, and seven of those cases had involved "'inappropriate' relationships."[5] The highly regarded former head of the Central Intelligence Agency, retired army general David Petraeus, resigned after an extramarital affair with his biographer was uncovered. In his statement announcing his resignation from the CIA, he said, "After being married for over 37 years, I showed extremely poor judgment by engaging in an extramarital affair . . . Such behavior is unacceptable, both as a husband and as the leader of an organization such as ours."[6] Cases involving senior officials receive media attention, but they are the tip of the iceberg when it comes to the problem of sexual misconduct in the military.

## Sexual Misconduct and Military Culture

In this chapter, sexual misconduct is an umbrella term that includes a range of behavior from the consensual yet prohibited sexual relationship with a subordinate to sexual assault and rape. In 2012, 26,000 active duty service members (6.1 percent of active duty women and 1.2 percent of active duty men) reported experiencing unwanted sexual contact.[7] Despite numerous studies, volumes of Congressional testimony, prevention plans, mandatory training, and the establishment of investigative special victim units, the problem of sexual misconduct remains part of the military social landscape.

The masculine ideal is well established in the military psyche: "It is not enough to simply be male; one must be 'more male' than the men in the next squad, platoon, and so forth."[8] Military culture can be described in part as male-dominated and infused with a warrior ethos that is characteristically masculine in nature and sometimes hostile to feminine identity. Such hostility is often manifested in crude cadence calls and profane references to those who do not epitomize the prevailing masculine ideal. Occasionally that hostility manifests as sexual violence. However, there is evidence that the existing social construction of what it means to be a warrior is undergoing change.

The lifting of the ban against the service of those who are openly gay or lesbian and the opening of specialties including combat roles to women are examples of unfolding change, but deep-seated cultures change slowly if at all, and social change is often accompanied by social friction. As L. Michael Allsep wrote in 2013 after the repeal of the "Don't Ask, Don't Tell" policy, "The difficulties still experienced by women in the armed forces 40 years after they were first incorporated in significant numbers indicates that this response will be insufficient to address the deeper cultural issues. Gender issues implicate deeply held beliefs and values that persist even in the face of years of official admonishment and denial."[9]

Sex scandals are perennial features at the military service academies. Military service academies are hybrid structures. In many respects they are similar to non-military colleges and universities in that they confer baccalaureate degrees and are attended by a similar age demographic. In other ways they are significantly different from their civilian counterparts. They are considered military institutions with martial ideals and culture, and students are subject to the Uniform Code of Military Justice. As a result, reports of sexual misconduct are inconsistent with public expectations about what is to be expected from institutions of such status. After a series of sex scandals involving cadets and midshipmen, Congress mandated an annual report on sexual harassment and violence at the military service academies. The findings included the observation that those in positions of authority apparently take the problem seriously by responding to allegations when received, but they have also struggled to deal with cadets and midshipmen who disregard academy policies by targeting others for gender-related misbehavior.

The problem is compounded when fellow cadets are complicit in or condone the misbehavior. The 2012–2013 Department of Defense report counted seventy reports of sexual assault.[10] Some of the complaints involved incidents that occurred prior to military service, but most involved cadet on cadet misconduct. According to one study, incidents of sexual assault are higher on civilian college campuses: one in five women in college is sexually assaulted.[11] But that fact is of little solace; as with civilian colleges and institutions, the offenses in military academies are underreported. Only about 11 percent of the cadets and midshipmen who indicated having experienced unwanted sexual contact actually reported a sexual assault.[12]

Sexual assault in the military is both prevalent and significantly underreported. The respondents in a 2012 Department of Defense study indicated that of 26,000 incidents of unwanted sexual contact only 3,374 were reported.[13] A qualitative study by Burns and colleagues of women deployed to combat zones examined the dynamics that contribute to sexual assault during deployments and the reasons why women decide not to report assaults.[14] They identified deployment dynamics as contributing factors, including long-duration deployments, deprivation of sexual activity, high-risk behaviors such as excessive alcohol consumption, high stress levels, and changes in the perception of "normal" behavior that sometimes occur in a war zone. Military culture was identified as a contributing factor, specifically the presence of sexual hostility, low representation of women, and the dynamics of rank and power. Some victims believed that unit leaders turned a blind eye to sex offenses: as a result there were few consequences for perpetrators, and victims were frequently blamed as the source of the problem. Unit cohesion served as a double-edged sword in that some unit climates were supportive of reporting while in others the pressure to maintain cohesion discouraged it.[15] Concerns about lack of confidentiality, lack of knowledge, not wanting to report, and the presence of stigma or shame were identified as additional barriers to reporting.

When those who are assaulted do come forward, they sometimes feel revictimized by the investigative process. Even sensitive and caring investigators can telegraph that the victim is not believed merely by the kinds of questions they must ask. This adds to a sense of isolation and suspicion that the victim's complaint will not be addressed. Complainants are typically advised of their Article 31 rights, the military equivalent of a Miranda warning, even though they are not in custody or suspected of committing an offense. Such rights warnings infer that the complainant has done something wrong—a presupposition that a victim is lying. Traumatized victims do not always remember the details of an attack clearly, and discrepancies in their initial statements contribute to a lack of credibility that can halt an investigation or hinder subsequent prosecution. If they are perceived as submitting a false statement, complainants can be charged with a criminal offense.

Military organizations have been slow to partner with the rape crisis centers that exist in many communities near military installations, which can provide emotional support to victims throughout the investigative process. Sexual assault investigations are challenging for even the most experienced and well-trained investigators, and many do not have extensive experience in dealing with victims of sexual assault. Trials are another point where victims feel revictimized as they must testify to the details of the incident in open court and undergo cross-examination by the defense.

In an attempt at quality control through the application of objective standards to written case notes and files, a 2013 report by the Department of Defense Inspector General evaluated 501 sexual assault investigations conducted by military criminal investigative organizations from across the services.[16] Each service publishes policies addressing how sexual assault investigations are to be conducted, but the inspectors noted that those policies tended to vary. Each agency had its own standards and methods for conducting records checks, transmitting files, and including agent case notes to name a few. The reviewers noted that 11 percent of cases had significant deficiencies, and some were returned to the agencies for additional investigative effort. The Naval Criminal Investigative Service could not locate two investigative reports, which were presumed to be lost in transit between a field office and higher headquarters. Other significant case deficiencies included:

- Key evidence was not collected from the crime scene, the victim, or the subject.
- Crime scene examinations were not completed, not completed thoroughly, or not completed before the loss of crucial evidence.
- Witness interviews were not thorough or not conducted.

- Subject or victim interviews were not thorough or reinterviews of subject or victims did not sufficiently develop new information.[17]

To date, no reviews have addressed the opinions of victims and witnesses, so there is no assessment as to the degree to which the targets of sexual assault were satisfied or dissatisfied with their treatment during the investigative process. The review did include an analysis of the relationships between victims and perpetrators:

> For 531 victims, a relationship of some type (acquaintance, friend, or co-worker) existed between the victims and the subjects. In the majority of cases, the subjects were acquaintances (160 of 531, or 30 percent) or friends (110 of 531, or 21 percent) of the victim. In some instances (55 of 531, or 10 percent), the subject was identified as a coworker of the victim. In 82 instances of 531 (15 percent), the subject was unknown to the victim or had no identified relationship with them.[18]

When the perpetrator was in the military, the report identified the nature of the relationship with their victims.

- In twenty-two instances, the subject was the victim's supervisor; in rare instances, four of 531, the subject was subordinate to the victim.
- In one instance, the subject was the victim's roommate.
- In five instances, the subject was identified as the victim's recruiter.
- In one instance, the subject was the victim's instructor.[19]

Because of the significant power differentials in military organizations, sexual relationships between superiors and subordinates are categorically prohibited, and such relationships within the chain of command are punishable even if they are ostensibly consensual. Restrictions that intrude into the bedroom of consenting adults might seem anachronistic and unwarranted to some, but any specter of a superior preying on a subordinate or a subordinate's family members has an obvious destructive impact on good order and discipline. Those who use their position of status, power, and authority to gain sexual favors are viewed as unsavory and dishonorable.

The periodic scandals in training settings and reactions to them are demonstrative. In 1996 allegations surfaced that cadre at the Aberdeen Proving Ground in Maryland misused the power of their positions to obtain sexual favors from trainees. They engaged in predatory behavior, including the sharing of information about trainees who might be susceptible or vulnerable. The allegations received national media attention, and the army responded with a number of rule changes and policy interventions, including mandatory training on sexual harassment. Central to the prosecution phase was the notion of constructive force, which asserts consent is not possible when there is a significant disparity in power between the participants. When applying the notion of constructive force, any sexual conduct between drill sergeants and those in their charge is considered as taking place without the consent of the trainee. The Aberdeen case resulted in several prosecutions, including a sentence to twenty-five years' hard labor for eighteen counts of rape and other offenses.

Before the Aberdeen case was concluded, the army's top enlisted soldier was accused of sexually harassing some of his subordinates. A similar scandal broke in 2013 at Lackland Air Force Base in San Antonio, Texas. Eventually thirty-five instructors were relieved of duties, the commander of the squadron was removed, and seventeen instructors were accused of criminal offenses with some receiving lengthy prison terms.

In the wake of such publicly disappointing events, institutional responses typically involve implementation of accountability measures including removal of those in authoritative positions, additional mandatory training, a rush to policy change, and studies or blue ribbon panels. There is typically little policy change outside of periods of crisis response.

## Congressional Interventions

In 2012 a military court-martial convicted an air force lieutenant colonel, who served as an inspector general, of aggravated sexual assault and sentenced him to a year of confinement and dismissal. A three-star general later overturned the conviction and reinstated the officer. The military justice system gives commanders inordinate power in criminal cases, including the power to review the findings and sentences levied by courts-martial. At about the same time an officer who led the air force sexual assault response team was accused of groping a woman outside a bar in Virginia. He was later acquitted for misdemeanor assault, but the incident sparked widespread concern over the military's ability to deal with sex offenses. The Senate Armed Services Committee launched a series of hearings that included poignant testimony by military victims of sexual assault.

All the victims of sexual assault who testified at the 2013 Senate hearings were compelling, but the testimony of Rebekah Havrilla was particularly noteworthy not only because of the awful specifics of her case but also because her experience is representative of many others.

My deployment brought more than just the stress of occupational hazards. During my tour, one of my team leaders continuously sexually harassed me and was sexually abusive towards me. This behavior caused me so much anxiety that I ended up self-referring to mental health and on medication to manage not just the stress of my deployment, but also the stress of having to live with an abusive leader and co-worker. One week before my unit was scheduled to return back to the United States, I was raped by another service member that had worked with our team. Initially, I chose not to do a report of any kind because I had no faith in my chain of command as my first sergeant previously had sexual harassment accusations against him and the unit climate was extremely sexist and hostile in nature towards women. After disclosing my rape to a few close friends, I ended up filing a restricted report sixty days before I left active duty against both my rapist and my team leader, but had no intentions of ever doing a formal investigation.

I began a job as a contractor and entered the Reserves at Fort Leonard Wood, MO and tried to start a different life for myself. Reintegration was challenging and I had few support systems to rely on. I struggled with depression and the effects of Post-Traumatic Stress. Approximately a year after separating from active duty, I was on orders for job training and during that time I ran into my rapist in a post store. He recognized me and told me that he was stationed on the same installation. I was so re-traumatized from the unexpectedness of seeing him that I removed myself from training and immediately sought out assistance from an Army chaplain who told me among other things, that the rape was god's will and that god was trying to get my attention so that I would go back to church. Again, I did not file an unrestricted report against my rapist.

Six months later, a friend called me and told me they had found pictures of me online that my perpetrator had taken during my rape. At that point, I felt that my rape was always going to haunt me unless I did something about it so I went to Army Criminal Investigation Division (CID) and a full investigation was completed. The initial CID interview was the most humiliating thing that I have ever experienced. I had to relive the entire event for over four hours with a male CID agent whom I had never met and explain to him repeatedly exactly what was happening in each one of the pictures that were found. After the interview was completed, I heard nothing from the investigator until four months later when CID requested that I come back in to repeat my statement to a new investigator who was taking over my case. I almost refused. During the four months of waiting without any word on the case except phone calls from my friends who had been interviewed, I lived in constant fear that I might run into my rapist again or that he might retaliate against me in some way. I decided to continue with the case even though I felt that nothing was ever going to be resolved and six months later, I was told that even though my rapist had admitted to having "consensual" sex with me while married, his chain of command refused to pursue any charges of adultery and the case was closed.

The military criminal justice system is broken. Unfortunately, my case is not much different from the many other cases that have been reported. I feared retaliation before and after I reported, the investigative process severely re-traumatized me, many of the institutional systems set up to help failed me miserably, my perpetrator went unpunished despite admitting to a crime against the UCMJ, and commanders were never held accountable for making the choice to do nothing.[20]

A former navy petty officer Brian K. Lewis also testified before the committee. His case was unique as a male victim of sexual assault. His testimony served to highlight problems faced by male victims. Women are significantly more likely to be sexually assaulted, but they comprise a smaller percentage of the force—in terms of total numbers, the majority of those who are sexually assaulted are believed to be men.[21] He reported being raped by a superior noncommissioned officer and testified that he was ordered by the command not to report the incident to the Naval Criminal Investigative Service. He was diagnosed with a personality disorder and medically discharged, a characterization and diagnosis he contends were false. He subsequently received a 100 percent disability rating from the Veterans Administration for post-traumatic stress disorder. He pointed out that sexual assault is not just about sex but also about violence, power, and sometimes abuse of authority.

The reforms haven't worked because they have targeted the symptoms of this epidemic. They have not addressed the root cause, which is that the military justice system is fraught with inherent personal bias, conflict of interest, abuse of authority and too often a low regard for the victim. While civilians have the constitutional protections of an independent judicial system, service-members do not. Service-members must report rape to their commanders. However, if their commanders take action and prove that rape occurred, they also prove a failure of their own leadership.

It is only natural for commanders to want to believe that a crime did not happen. Making it disappear entails less risk for their careers. And, not pursuing prosecution is much less disruptive for their units. Commanders know and work with the people involved, therefore they have biases. All those within the military hierarchy have strong incentives to follow their commanders' biases. Commanders have tremendous power over the lives and future careers of those in their command. It is only natural that survivors experience repeated patterns of cover-up and retaliation. No wonder Congress' reforms have not successfully delivered justice within a military justice system governed by commanders who have strong incentives not to bring rape to justice.

According to DoD, 51% of male victims report that the perpetrator is of higher rank and 26% report that the perpetrator is actually in their chain of command. And 62% of female victims report that the perpetrator is of higher rank and 23% report that the perpetrator is actually in their chain of command.

Congress, through the UCMJ, put commanders in charge of violent sexual crime—from victim care, through the legal and investigative processes these cases involve. Commanders have too often failed to care for the victim or prosecute the perpetrator. They have failed to end this long standing epidemic.

The quest for a quick resolution or an affinity for the defendant sometimes leads the command to reduce sentences, grant clemency or overturn convictions. These decisions are some of the reasons why 86% of victims do not report.[22]

Havrilla and Lewis both blamed military leaders for failing to take appropriate action after reports of sexual assault. Such behavior contributed to their sense of isolation and betrayal. While Havrilla pointed to the investigative process as a source of revictimization, Lewis focused his testimony on the role of the military medical system.

Another form of victim blaming comes from military doctors. Under pressure from commands, doctors often diagnose survivors with personality or similar disorders, as a way to discharge survivors from the service. Survivors of MST [military sexual trauma] need to be treated equally with combat troops suffering from PTSD. This means that the ban on Personality Disorder discharges currently in effect should be extended throughout DoD to include survivors of military sexual trauma. Personality Disorders, by definition, cannot come about as the result of a rape. Military doctors need to be held accountable for these false diagnoses. Such weaponizing diagnoses are unfair and unjust to our service men and women who have been victims of sexual assault in our military.[23]

For a while it appeared that measures to significantly overhaul the military justice system were imminent, including the possibility of removing commanders' review authority and moving sexual assault offenses into civilian courts. In the end Congress passed significant but more modest changes that required the appointment of judge advocates to serve as Article 32 investigating officers where practicable. Article 32 hearings are the military equivalent of a grand jury proceeding. The law also required the appointment of special victims counsel to ensure the rights of the victim are protected. The convening authority can no longer adjust any findings of guilt for felony offenses where the sentence is longer than six months or contains a discharge. They cannot change findings for any sex crime, irrespective of sentencing time. The five-year statute of limitations on rape and sexual assault was also removed, and commanders must immediately report allegations of sexual assault to military criminal investigative agencies.

## Why Do They Do It?

Why do those who have long periods of exemplary service and a history of temperate behavior seemingly lose their minds and engage in sexual conduct that results in catastrophic personal and professional loss as well as harm to the institutions they have ably served? Conventional wisdom holds that they make a rational and calculated decision to satisfy a short-term desire, without considering the likelihood of getting caught and the resulting negative impact. Another prevailing hypothesis holds that they are fundamentally morally flawed, possessing character deficiencies. Terry Price offers another suggestion, that some leaders come to perceive the satisfaction of their own needs and desires as outweighing other considerations because they are such exceptional people.[24] What is good for them therefore becomes perceived as in the interest of the group. "In other words, when leaders come to an exaggerated view of just how special they really are, they can conclude that they are justified in making self-interested exceptions of themselves that would not be justified for others in their group, organizations, or society."[25] If Price is correct, there is a rather obvious connection between narcissism and those with a propensity to engage in risky sexual relationships. With their needs and desires elevated to preeminence, a lack of self-awareness, increased impulsivity, and lack of consideration for others can combine to set the stage for unethical and ultimately destructive conduct.

Ludwig and Longenecker identified a pattern in ethical violations by those in powerful positions who were otherwise very successful. In allusion to the biblical story of King David and Bathsheba, they termed it the Bathsheba syndrome.[26] The story begins with David, a powerful and successful king, sending a subordinate to lead the Israelite army against the Ammonites. Typically the place of the king was with the army in the field, but David decided to remain in Jerusalem—maybe he was tired and felt entitled to a break. From his rooms high in the palace he saw a beautiful woman bathing. He contrived to learn more about her and discovered her name was Bathsheba, the wife of Uriah, one of David's soldiers. He called her to him, slept with her, and later she sent word to notify him that she was pregnant. David devised a plan to cover up his transgression: he called Uriah back to Jerusalem to sleep with Bathsheba in hopes he would believe the child was his. However, Uriah refused to enter his house or make love to his wife while his soldiers were in the field. So then David devised a plan that put Uriah on the frontline where the fighting was the fiercest, resulting in his death. After a period of mourning, David took Bathsheba as his queen. The child she bore later died, and David faced a series of calamities. From this story, Ludwig and Longenecker derived a series of observations that seems to stand the test of time.

David came from humble beginnings and experienced a remarkable rise to power. He was perceived as righteous and was popular with his people. He knew right from wrong, possessed many talents, and yet still engaged in behavior that made him the central player in a cautionary tale of lust and abandonment of principles. Ludwig and Longenecker suggest that success brings privileged access to resources. In David's case it was his vantage point from the roof of the palace that provided him with the opportunity to observe Bathsheba as she bathed. Military leaders have access to funds, perquisites, power to reward and punish, personnel who want to please them, information, and other resources that those of lesser status in the organization do not have. Such access is appropriate and necessary to provide them with means to act in the interests of the organization, not to achieve their personal desires. However, as mentioned in the previous chapter, some ineffective leaders have difficulty in distinguishing the difference between organizational and personal assets.

Part of David's problem stemmed from his extraordinary success, which gave him an inflated perception of self-worth and ability. He also overestimated his power, believing that he could successfully cover up his transgression; his decision took a bad case of infidelity and compounded it with an even worse case of homicide. Attempting to cover up a transgression is an especially bad idea in public-sector organizations. Some astute observers always begin with the presumption that cover-ups are under way and that the truth is likely to emerge eventually. Attempts to engage in cover-ups invariably backfire and tend to amplify the resulting level of distrust and lack of confidence.

The best approach to a transgression is to completely disclose it, in all its ugly glory, and focus on establishing measures to ensure it is not repeated in the future. Those with an inflated ego seem to believe that they are entitled to sexual escapades, believe they are clever enough to get away with it, and have sufficient power to cover it up if discovered. Like David, they are frequently wrong on all counts.

The lives of those who bear great responsibility are not easy, despite the benefits that accrue with higher status. Such leaders often spend long hours away from home, have workaholic tendencies, and are frequently isolated. They experience high-stress conditions for prolonged periods. To a degree, they can become hooked on success, with an accompanying fear of failure that produces a level of anxiety that is physically and emotionally taxing. A lack of intimacy and an expanded ego plus a sense of entitlement lead to a drive toward unethical choices.[27] To address the Bathsheba syndrome, Ludwig and Longenecker suggest seven lessons:

1. Leaders are in their positions to focus on doing what is right for their organization's short-term and long-term success. This can't happen if they aren't where they are supposed to be, doing what they are supposed to be doing.
2. There will always be temptations that come in a variety of shapes and forms that will prompt leaders to make decisions they know they shouldn't make. With success will come additional ethical trials.
3. Perpetrating an unethical act is a personal conscious choice on the part of the leader that frequently places a greater

emphasis on personal gratification rather than on the organization's needs.

4. It is difficult if not impossible to partake in unethical behavior without implicating and/or involving others in the organization.

5. Attempts to cover-up unethical practices can have dire organizational consequences, including innocent people getting hurt, power being abused, trust being violated, other individuals being corrupted, and needed resources being diverted.

6. Not getting caught initially can produce self-delusion and increase the likelihood of future unethical behavior.

7. Getting caught can destroy the leader, the organization, innocent people, and everything the leader has spent his or her life working for.[28]

Linsky and Heifetz fully recognize the power of the human need for intimacy and delight as well as the risks of falling prey to a lack of self-knowledge and self-discipline.

We all have hungers, which are expressions of our normal human needs. But sometimes those hungers disrupt our capacity to act wisely or purposefully. Perhaps one of our needs is too great and renders us as vulnerable. Perhaps the setting in which we operate exaggerates our normal level of need, amplifying our desires and overwhelming our self-controls. Or, our hungers might be unchecked simply because our human needs are not being met in our personal lives . . . Yet each of these normal human needs can get us into trouble when we lose the personal wisdom and discipline required to manage them productively and fulfill them appropriately.[29]

Linsky and Heifetz do not suggest that leaders should altogether deny fundamental human drives lest they manifest in other more destructive ways. Instead they suggest the channeling of desire for intimacy and close human contact into productive and appropriate relationships. Those relationships sometimes require work to maintain in a healthy state, but they are a worthy investment of time and effort.

Leaders should clearly distinguish in their own minds the difference between the role they play in an organization and themselves as individuals. Sometimes leaders need to remind themselves that they really aren't that funny just because everyone laughs at their jokes, and that they are not irresistible to the opposite sex just because attractive people pay attention to them. People who are tired and emotionally exhausted or under the influence of alcohol are prone to engaging in destructive behavior. "When people look to a man as someone special, it sometimes inflates appetite as well as ego. So some men in this needy state, end up engaging in sexual activity that crosses boundaries inappropriately doing damage to themselves, their issues, and the workplace."[30] The management of hungers is not just an issue for men. Women leaders sometimes find it difficult to disengage from their professional role at the end of the day and relax into emotional and sexual intimacy.[31] People are also attracted to women in power, and being looked at in a special way can also enhance a woman's hunger for intimacy and companionship.

Perhaps military leaders are not prepared particularly well to deal with the temptations that come with success. There is ample evidence that engaging in sexual misconduct is wrong and brings severe personal and professional ramifications. Countless examples drive that message home. Yet threat briefings and severe penalties do not seem to be very effective in preventing sexual misconduct, and a review of the curriculum of joint and service school curriculums reveals little that would be useful in addressing the topic. Perhaps those in demanding leadership positions need additional insights and preparation to properly manage their legitimate human needs for sex and intimacy.

### It's Not Only a Matter of Character

Aristotle believed that character is derived from habituating virtuous behavior through emulation of good examples, and those of good character can be relied upon to be consistently honorable in the face of all manner of temptation. This concept of character development has been a mainstay of service academies that endeavor to produce responsible leaders. The mission of the U.S. Military Academy is "To educate, train, and inspire the Corps of Cadets so that each graduate is a commissioned leader of character committed to the values of Duty, Honor, Country; and prepared for a career of professional excellence and service to the Nation as an officer in the United States Army."[32] Much of the contemporary ethics talk in military organizations has centered on concepts of character and integrity. The military's overreliance on the notion of character could be a contributing factor to the problem of sexual misconduct.

There is little evidence that we are particularly effective at developing good character in adults whose basis of morality was established at a young age. We are also learning through the tools of modern social psychology and experimental ethics that human behavior is far more a function of situational and contingent factors than we might otherwise like to believe. Even otherwise good people will apparently do bad things under specific conditions. Those who are upstanding and virtuous at one point in time might engage in blameworthy behavior at another. Those who are exemplary in some aspects of their lives can be reprehensible in others.

Randall H. "Duke" Cunningham was a naval flight officer for twenty years, was one of the only combat aces of the Vietnam War, was awarded two silver stars, the Navy Cross, and the Air Medal, and was an instructor at the U.S. Navy's Fighter Weapons School. He was admired and respected, and he was elected to Congress where he served for fourteen years—until he was convicted of accepting 2.4 million dollars in bribes from a defense contractor in exchange for lucrative defense contracts.[33] This case demonstrates the ethereal nature of character. Some might assert that Cunningham had suffered character flaws all along; if that is the case, they only became apparent in retrospect, as he successfully completed a full military career and rose to a position of considerable trust and responsibility before those flaws were unmasked. Or perhaps at varying times of his life he had acted both honorably and dishonorably. Or perhaps his case is a contemporary example of the Bathsheba syndrome. An emphasis on character alone puts the locus of control solely on the individual. Although focusing on individual character can be helpful and even proper to a degree, an excessive focus on character alone can divert attention from other variables worthy of attention. For example, a person of good character would not be expected to engage in misconduct merely because he or she consumed alcoholic beverages, yet alcohol consumption is frequently associated with sexual misconduct. And if good character were the only variable that can be relied upon to prevent sexual misconduct, there would be no need to focus on helping leaders derive healthy and satisfying relationships to meet their intimacy needs or increase their levels of self-awareness. Experience tells us that systemic problems involving complex human social systems are rarely by addressed by simple, one-dimensional solutions.

When leaders come to perceive of themselves as special and entitled to exceptions not afforded to others in the organization or are unprepared for the inevitable temptations of success, they become vulnerable and part of the problem. Leaders who fail to execute their responsibilities to prevent sexual misconduct or respond appropriately when such incidents do occur are complicit in its continuation. Just as absentee or laissez-faire leadership styles provide opportunities for toxic leaders to thrive, moribund leadership serves to perpetuate the problem of sexual misconduct.

# 6 Surviving a Toxic Leader

> It is not power that corrupts but fear. Fear of losing power corrupts those who wield it and fear of the scourge of power corrupts those who are subject to it.
>
> —Aung San Suu Kyi

Nobody aspires to become the father confessor of hundreds of service members who suffer at the hands of bad leaders, but after the publication of several articles on the subject, the calls and letters flowed in and continue to this day. The stories were both disappointing and heartbreaking, recounting misplaced faith and confidence and feelings of hopelessness, bitterness, and betrayal. In some cases the abuse was ongoing; others were licking their wounds and retrospectively analyzing traumatic experiences. They all bore figurative scars. They were frequently disoriented and shaken.

Some tried to avoid blaming the army, navy, air force, or marine corps, but they were often resentful that the organization they otherwise so enjoyed serving would treat them so shabbily. Most had no idea why they were targeted for abuse; others were particularly self-aware and had ideas about how their behavior might have contributed to the situation. A few were able to laugh about their experiences with bad leadership and saw them as part of their growth and development; in a social setting they would sometimes speak of their experiences with toxic leaders almost with a sense of pride: "That's not so bad," one would invariably remark, "Let me tell you about the son of a bitch I once worked for."

In most cases the suffering subordinates felt isolated and alone, as if they were the only ones to have had these experiences. And in most cases they were searching for information on how to deal with the situation or make some sense of what had happened to them.

## Advice for Suffering Subordinates

Giving helpful advice is difficult without a thorough understanding of each situation because no two are exactly alike. Even with a clear understanding of the details, advice and armchair theorizing are no substitutes for counseling, therapy, or legal services that the victims would most benefit from. Some do seek mental health services and receive treatment, but they are the minority. There is no simple formula for dealing with a toxic leader, and every individual case is exceptional. However, over many cases one can observe certain patterns that tend to be true more often than not, and from those patterns come rules of thumb that can be helpful in weathering difficult situations. The more that is understood about this phenomenon, the more tools and tactics are available to those who are attempting to survive it.

Why don't we simply withhold followership from toxic leaders? Why do we seem to so willingly support those who are destructive and corrupt? According to Jean Lipman-Blumen, one of the most thoughtful authors on the subject of toxic leadership, we actually seem to prefer toxic leaders and elevate them to positions of responsibility over those who are not toxic—a discomforting assertion.[1] The military environment is one where leadership, authority, and power are tightly woven. The power differentials are significant, and discipline and loyalty are prized concepts. The system of superordination and subordination is reinforced by both culture and legal code. Leadership might well be a voluntary process in theory, but withholding followership is not a healthy option for most service members. Article 94 of the Uniform Code of Military Justice defines the offense of mutiny as any person subject to the code "who with intent to usurp or override lawful military authority, refuses, in concert with any other person, to obey orders or otherwise do his duty or creates any violence or disturbance."[2] The offense is punishable by death or such other punishment as a court-martial directs. Failure to obey a lawful order or regulation is also punishable under the code under Article 92. Undermining those in positions of authority even if they are toxic is seriously frowned upon in the military.

The popular literature has no shortage of bad advice on the subject of toxic leaders, but it often fails to take into account the unique context of the military. For example, the advice to treat toxic leaders like bullies on the playground by directly confronting them and telling them that under no circumstances will their behavior be tolerated might work in the fifth grade, but a truly toxic boss will see such behavior as an insubordinate affront to their authority. When threatened in such a manner, they will typically seek to use the considerable means at their disposal to destroy the subordinate. In the private sector the arbiter of workplace conflict and complaints is the human resources office, but that has no equivalent in the military environment. Uniformed personnel cannot just walk off the job or mount a revolt to overthrow their supervisors.

James (a pseudonym) had recently assumed command of a reserve battalion. He was excited to present his first training plan to the brigade commander after he and his staff put considerable thought and effort into its preparation. They all wanted to get off on the right foot with the new boss. That was a hope that would remain unfulfilled. After the presentation and in front of the brigade staff, the toxic boss expressed nonspecific dissatisfaction with the product and launched into an angry tirade, questioning James's competence and integrity. James left the meeting surprised, embarrassed, and angry. He prepared a lengthy, angry e-mail to his boss wherein he objected to such treatment and outlined his expectations with regard to being treated with respect and dignity in the future. This was not a good idea: if a confrontation is inevitable, it should be conducted face to face and behind closed doors at a time of careful choosing. Although an e-mail message provides a record of the communication, it is not likely to garner respect from the toxic leader. At their next meeting the brigade commander demanded a list of every soldier who had missed a drill since James assumed command, the reasons for those absences, and annotations of corrective action taken. Of course the timeline to provide the requested information was unreasonable. The battle was under way.

If there is a gradation of toxic leadership from those who occasionally manifest toxic tendencies to the malevolently gleeful destroyer of careers, it follows that different approaches are appropriate for varying levels of toxicity. Those at the extreme and destructive end of the spectrum might not be approachable at all, but many who exhibit problematic behaviors can be reached, given the right circumstances at the right time and place. Robert Sutton observes that some toxic behavior is unintentional: "They don't mean to be assholes. They might be surprised if you gently let them know they are leaving you feeling belittled and demeaned."[3] It may take patience and a keen eye to discern the right time to broach the subject, and it may take the skills of a diplomat to address the issue tactfully, but being a good follower includes the obligation to try.

The best time to approach the subject is when the boss is relaxed, rested, confident, and perhaps even reflective. It's best to avoid times when either party is agitated or angry, to have the conversation in private, and to maintain a strong overtone of respect. Linnda Durré has provided some general guidelines for handling a toxic boss in the private sector; although not all her suggestions are applicable in a military setting, a few can be modified to translate pretty well.

- Know what your issues are. Make a list of exactly what you want to say, and keep the notes with you when you have the meeting. Nervousness and anxiety make us forget what we want to say, and the notes can help us remember.
- Rehearse the conversation in front of a mirror or with a friend. Ask your friend for feedback. Try audio- or video-taping yourself so that you can hear and see how you sound and what you look like. Critique your own performance. Do it again and again until you feel comfortable. In the letter or the e-mail or when you speak to your boss in person, ask when a good time would be to discuss your issues.
- Turn off cell phones and office phones, let the boss say what he or she has to say, and then respond. Keep everything confidential. State that your intention is to have a win-win outcome, that you are open to hearing what your boss has to say, and that you want to resolve this amiably.
- Act professionally, stand up straight with shoulders back, and use a pleasant tone of voice, not in a bullying stance or tone or a whining-victim stance or tone. Use solid eye contact—do not look off at the ceiling or the floor. Say what you mean, and mean what you say. Know what you have control over and what you don't. Don't give ultimatums if you can't back them up with action. Be prepared to be fired.
- Start out positively and give compliments, state what negative issues need to be addressed, and end positively with a statement that you want to resolve the situation.
- Don't attack or blame. Keep the communication as a calm description of a certain behavior that he or she does, how it affects you, and how you would like it to be. Use "I" statements—"I feel this way when you do that," or "When you say or do that, it makes me feel this way." Always own your reactions and perceptions. If the boss says, "Other people don't feel that way . . ." simply keep on track by saying something along the lines of "But it's how I feel, and I need to tell you and get it resolved."

- Give clear, simple solutions—"I'd prefer it if you would do this"—and be very specific on how and in what ways you would like the behavior to change.[4]

## The Safest Path

The sad truth of the matter is that the safest course of action when confronted with a toxic leader is to suffer in silence or seek an expeditious exit. Leadership positions rotate frequently due to the inevitable personnel churn that is characteristic of military personnel systems, so it is likely that either the leader or subordinate will rotate before long. Volunteering for schools, courses, or other assignments can sometimes limit the amount of contact or expedite a departure. In the meantime a social support system can be of benefit, consisting of trusted agents, a mentor, friends, and even close family members. Sometimes there are other trustworthy enlightened leaders around who are genuinely concerned about the welfare of the organization and the people in it. Carefully reach out to them as potential allies.[5]

Those suffering under a toxic leader need not be isolated and alone, but they should avoid venting to or in front of subordinates. They are not likely to appreciate a whining supervisor, and such talk inevitably gets back to the boss.

Waiting it out under a toxic leader can be an exhausting endeavor, and prolonged exposure to stress has serious health implications. Stress reduction and resiliency techniques, a healthy diet, and a focus on physical fitness can be most beneficial. Exposure to the toxic leader should be limited to the maximum extent possible. Sutton suggests practicing emotional detachment and refusing to let the supervisor's vicious words and deeds touch your soul—a state he describes as "comfortably numb"—until you find a workplace worthy of your full passion and commitment.[6] Marcia Whicker suggests taking a long-run view of petty slights and actions and ignoring them whenever possible.[7]

Most importantly, do not emulate the toxic behavior or focus your displaced anger on your own subordinates or family members. Harvey Hornstein points out that a brutal boss's subordinates are not justified in or excused for mistreating others just because they suffer abuse.[8] It might help to consider the observation that "toxic leaders are fundamentally flawed and will eventually self-destruct."[9] Although you shouldn't count on justice or karmic forces to intervene during your tenure, keep in mind that what goes around comes around eventually.

An officer who was involved in setting up and running promotion boards related an experience that indicates there is some justice in the world. A notoriously toxic colonel was up for promotion to brigadier general. He had powerful sponsors, had all the right assignments, and according to fitness reports and evaluations filed by his superiors his duty performance was exemplary. His impact on others was no secret in the field, but there was nothing in the official record that would indicate a problem. The board administrator knew of the officer and his reputation and had even experienced his toxic style firsthand. As the files on the candidates were being passed out one of the board members turned to the administrator and asked, "Hey, this one is from your career field. What do you think?" That presented an ethical dilemma for the administrator, who was under oath to ensure the proper running of the board without influencing its decisions. The officer demurred and then went into the hallway and slumped under the knowledge that the board might select the toxic leader for promotion and he could have stopped it. Later that day when collecting the files and materials after the voting was concluded, the administrator noticed that one board member wrote in bold letters on the file, "This officer has reached his station in life over the carcasses of his subordinates." He was not selected for promotion to the surprise of many. Sometimes the system works.

## Silver Linings

Although it is of little solace to the suffering, there are some positive outcomes associated with working for a bad boss. It can be a remarkable learning experience full of negative examples that are instructive in their own right. At the very least an astute observer can amass a long list of "things I will never do when I am in a position of authority." It is also beneficial to gain experience in working with those who are different, quirky, and even trying. There is no shortage of unusual people in this world to work for; building some tolerance for those who are dislikable or disagreeable is an exercise in patience and humility. Toxic leaders are often complicated people. Sometimes bright lights cast dark shadows. Learning to focus on those bright spots while minimizing the darker aspects of their personality is an exercise in optimism. Working for a toxic leader builds a form of interpersonal calluses. Once you have had close association with a human blowtorch, a boss with an occasionally poor attitude won't seem so bad. Those who survive a toxic leader are not likely to fall to pieces when their next boss has a bad day and barks at them.

## The Courageous and Risky Path

Sometimes the safest actions for an individual are not necessarily the best thing for the organization, but actions beyond suffering in silence and leaving bring increasing levels of personal risk. For example, a sergeant major who was scheduled to move on to another assignment and was eligible for retirement struggled with whether he should pursue a complaint against a toxic leader or just let bygones be bygones. He knew that filing a complaint would at the very least make him a powerful enemy, and those who cared about him tried to encourage him to take the safe path. His sense of decorum and self-preservation competed with his sense of professionalism and care for those left behind. He felt he would be letting the organization down by going quietly, so he was prepared to undergo an unpleasant departure if it might make a difference to those that remained in the unit.

Taking the complaint route, whether to the next level in the chain of command or to other grievance outlets, is a courageous act, and using the chain of command is an approach that is encouraged in all military organizations. Seeking an audience with the toxic supervisor's boss is a legitimate option that could provide relief, but the supplicant should understand that the toxic boss has easier access to his or her superiors: the boss can destroy subordinates' reputations long before they can obtain an audience to make their case. Remember that toxic leaders don't look so bad from the top down. The boss's boss might not see the negative impact ongoing below and might even appreciate aspects of the toxic leader's personality or performance. Also, it is easy for individuals to overestimate their importance to the organization. Who is a supervisor most invested in, their immediate subordinates or those two levels lower in the hierarchy? Removing a supervisor, especially a high ranking one, is not an action to be taken lightly. Even when justified due process is required, it creates a host of problems including the need to identify and move in a suitable off-cycle replacement.

In a developing case at an army installation, a battalion commander and her command sergeant major were temporarily relieved of command after an investigation described the commander as "a foul-mouthed boss who belittled soldiers, threw things during a meeting and sometimes stormed out of battalion gatherings."[10] Soldiers called the climate bad or worse, but the commander alleged that subordinates were confusing her passion with anger. A statement in the report from a captain in the unit was descriptive: "Her command style is toxic and it bleeds from the highest-ranking to the lowest promoting contention among all members of the unit."[11] She denied belittling others, claiming that she was making on-the-spot corrections and asserting that her critics were slackers. She said, "It seems that those who cannot meet the standard have the loudest voice."[12] The investigation recommended relief for cause, but a major general in the chain of command declined to remove the colonel and reinstated the command team. The reinstatement in this case seems a bit confusing, but considering the ramifications of a career-ending move, application of due process was appropriate. Perhaps the general was unconvinced by the evidence and as a matter of fundamental fairness felt she deserved to complete the career-enhancing command tour. After all, she could not have ascended to battalion command if she had not been effective in previous assignments, at least as determined by her prior supervisors. It doesn't take much imagination, however, to predict the reactions of members in the unit to the reinstatement. Those who had the courage to provide statements to the investigators likely felt some ambiguity and possibly anxiety about their relationship with the commander. However, at the very least the incident may have served as a needed wake-up call that prompted some reflection and changes in behavior, as appropriate for a person in a position of authority who learns that her actions are not having the intended positive effects.

Toxic leaders rarely see themselves as toxic or their behavior as destructive. They can lack an extraordinary amount of self-awareness and social sense. One of the world's most well-known executive coaches, Marshal Goldsmith, points out that all humans are to some degree delusional.[13] Some overestimate their impact in the world while others tend to underestimate their contributions and value. "They have no idea how their behavior is coming across to the people who matter—their bosses, colleagues, subordinates, customers, and clients."[14] When studying toxic leaders, it is usually necessary to obtain information about them from those in their orbit.

- They think they have all the answers, but others see it as arrogance.
- They think they're contributing to a situation with helpful comments, but others see it as butting in.
- They think they're delegating effectively, but others see it as shirking responsibilities.
- They think they're holding their tongue, but others see it as unresponsiveness.
- They think they're letting people think for themselves, but others see it as ignoring them.[15]

A small percentage of those in authoritative positions do understand the impact they have on others but just don't care. They are the psychopaths mentioned in Chapter 1. When working for a psychopath, appeals to their better nature are likely to fall on deaf ears—they don't have a better nature. Facilitated by the organizational dynamics described in the previous chapter, most toxic leaders have been rewarded for their behavior. In their mind their approach has been validated through promotion and selection to key leadership positions. They may receive indications that all is not well, but they are also quick to discard information that threatens their delusions and to accept information that validates their sense of self-importance. They typically avoid climate assessments, reject feedback from subordinates, and assiduously avoid most of the voluntary tools and instruments designed improve self-awareness. When forced to engage in psychological or feedback processes they are quick to dismiss or rationalize the results.

However, some enlightened commanders are receptive to complaints, and they will intervene with the toxic leader in order to develop or coach them to a more fruitful path. Consider the case of Kevin (another pseudonym). During a graduate seminar discussion on toxic leadership he boldly proclaimed himself to be a toxic leader. "But," he continued, "I had a good reason to be that way." Kevin had been placed in charge of an important function, and things were not going well. The team was generally viewed as dysfunctional, uncaring, and noncompliant. Upon assuming command of the organization Kevin's boss provided a grim analysis of the situation: Kevin's mission was to clean up the mess quickly, he was to use any means necessary to do so, and Kevin's boss promised his full support for any measures Kevin felt necessary. In his own words Kevin became "Tyrannosaurus Rex." He was utterly intolerant of poor performance, and was quick to fire, relieve, or reassign subordinates. He was loud and direct, and some even considered him brutal. Toxic leaders are often given nicknames by their followers, and Kevin's became "the Executioner." He confronted people with abandon and got their attention, and performance began to improve. They were responding out of fear, but the organization was showing some life.

After about nine months Kevin's boss provided another assessment. The organization had largely turned around and was doing a good job. "Now" he asked Kevin, "what are you going to do?" Initially stumped by the question, Kevin said, "I thought I was doing it." Kevin's supervisor patiently explained to him that the leadership style appropriate and necessary for a dysfunctional team was not appropriate for a high-performing team. The organization had changed, and it was now necessary for Kevin to make a change as well. His supervisor was quite direct and clear about what Kevin needed to do. First, he was instructed to convince his subordinates that he wasn't schizophrenic because they might not otherwise understand the dramatic change in their leader's behavior. He was tasked to explain the reasons for his previous behavior and his intention to adjust his style to a more appreciative and supportive approach. The dead weight that hampered the organization was now gone, and Kevin had a team that was worthy of nurturing and continued development. Kevin responded to the guidance, and the result was that both he and the organization thrived.

Commanders have the option of initiating an administrative investigation upon receipt of information about leadership behavior that is inconsistent with the underlying values of the organization. Sometimes that process provides the senior leader with information and documentation needed to justify an intervention, which can include removal from a leadership position. When toxic leaders are removed, subordinate reactions range from relief to celebration. However, it may be an ego-busting, humiliating, and tragic occurrence for the person getting sacked, and wounded bears are the most dangerous. If it turns out the allegations were unsubstantiated (or even if they are substantiated), complainants should not expect a warm reception.

Despite regulatory and legal protections to prevent retribution on whistle-blowers, often there is still a price to pay. An account that appeared in the *Air Force Times* provides a salient example.[16]

A colonel identified issues with personnel practices in the Air Force Reserve Command and sought a position that would give her an opportunity to implement change. Her name was at the top of a list of ten candidates for the director of the Active Guard and Reserve Management Office. A major general told others that he passed her over for the job because of her criticism of the system. An inspector general investigation found in favor of the colonel, substantiating that she had suffered retribution in violation of the federal military Whistleblower Protection Act. The investigation took eighteen months to complete, and by then her request to extend on active duty had been denied; she retired after twenty-three years of service. She alleged it was a forced retirement although an air force spokesman said she could have applied for another active guard and reserve position. Her assessment was that she "was never going to get another job . . . So I had to retire and he got to stay."[17] Although the general did receive a letter of reprimand for violating the Whistleblower Protection Act, he was allowed to remain in command.

When the chain of command is the problem or fails to respond to legitimate complaints, there are other official outlets for grievance. Every military organization and most federal agencies have an office of the inspector general that serves as the conscience of the organization, conducting inspections, assessments, and investigations. They are mostly interested in timely allegations of violations of the law, regulation, or policy. Mere disagreement with a leader's style or a personality conflict does not merit the initiation of an investigation, but cases of cruelty and maltreatment do fall within the purview of inspectors general. When behavior crosses into criminal conduct, as in the case of an assault, police or criminal investigative organizations (e.g., Air Force Office of Special Investigations, Naval Criminal Investigative Service, or United States Army Criminal Investigation Command) have jurisdiction, depending on the level of severity.

Inspector general investigations are typically thoroughly documented for the record. To facilitate the process, complainants should keep detailed notes with times, dates, and witnesses. Sutton recommends keeping an "asshole diary" to carefully document what happens and when.[18] (If you do keep such a document do not put "Asshole Diary" on the cover or filename or leave it on the desk or public drive for all to see.) Cases involving multiple complainants who are all willing to provide sworn testimony typically carry more weight than a lone complaint. Investigators prefer to hear from victims or witnesses who have personal knowledge or experience rather than those who heard about a transgression secondhand. Anonymous complaints typically have the lowest priority, and there is no guarantee they will receive much attention. Even toxic leaders are entitled to due process.

The Article 138 complaint process is a frequently overlooked option that provides an avenue of redress for an act or omission that is in violation of a law or regulation or beyond the legitimate authority of the commander. It provides a means to address unfairness or an abuse of power. The aggrieved person must submit the complaint in writing through the chain of command to the commander in question, so there is no option of anonymity. Article 138 complaints must be submitted within ninety days of the date the wrong was discovered. The commander has fifteen days to respond with corrective action or provide an interim response. Formal complaints are forwarded to the general court-martial convening authority, typically the commanding general, who appoints an investigating officer and applies corrective action. Eventually the complaint is reviewed at the service secretary level, and the findings are forwarded to the complainant. Those who think about filing an Article 138 complaint should consult a legal assistance attorney who can provide advice and assistance in drafting the complaint, and they can also enlist the assistance of a civilian attorney at their own expense.[19]

Members of the civilian workforce have additional avenues to present grievances, including access to their union representative if under a collective bargaining agreement. They can even pursue unfair labor practice complaints through federal agencies such as the U.S. Equal Employment Opportunity Commission in the case of discrimination or the courts if they can establish they were subjected to a hostile work environment. Civilian and military personal can both initiate congressional complaints to a senator or representative.

If the options presented in this book and others are unsatisfying to those working for a toxic leader, that is because there just aren't that many good answers. Some problems defy easy solution. The situations can be managed for better or worse, but good outcomes are not guaranteed. We might as well acknowledge that those who wind up under a toxic leader have drawn a bad hand. A particularly wise field grade officer once provided a young lieutenant with this sage advice: "At some point in your career you are going to run up against an asshole for a boss. Whether you have a long or short military career will depend on how you navigate that situation."

The best approach to dealing with toxic leaders is not by individual action by less powerful subordinates, but through systemic and organizational approaches that identify and remediate the unhealthy dynamics that allow toxic leaders to exist and multiply.[20] World-class organizations like the U.S. military and those who aspire to be great should put into place mechanisms to detect the presence of toxic leaders and then attempt to develop them out of their toxic behaviors or remove them from positions where they can harm others. The burden is too great for subordinates, dedicated and loyal as they might be. They just do not have the power, status, and prestige to pull it off.

A brilliant and hardworking scientist was appreciated for his many contributions to the organization and as a result of his significant technical abilities he was placed in charge of a team of scientists. That is when the trouble began. He enjoyed working in the laboratory, but he did not enjoy leading. He wasn't good at being a supervisor and could not understand why he couldn't just tell people what to do and be done with it. The complaints and dissatisfaction began to mount, and the company eventually decided to remove him from a supervisory position: they contrived a "super technical" position where his talents could still benefit the organization without the interpersonal damage. He was pleased with the change, and his former team was relieved.

Organizations make the mistake of conflating technical ability with leadership skill on a regular basis. Nothing in a scientist's job skills, knowledge, and abilities statement indicate interpersonal skill or emotional intelligence as conditions of employment. Great classroom teachers are sometimes pushed into administration and make lousy principals; outstanding beat cops can become mediocre sergeants; and talented engineers are occasionally confounded by personnel problems they encounter when placed in charge of a team. The formulas they like to rely upon seem to defy application to complex human social systems. As one laboratory supervisor put it, "If our scientists were people persons they wouldn't be sitting around all day with their faces in a microscope now would they?"

If psychological type theory is correct, personalities are hard wired and do not change much, absent some form of trauma or pathology, but behavior can be modified. At a leader development course the then commander of U.S. Southern Command, General James T. Hill, addressed a group of colonels and GS-15 civilian employees. He told them that he understood that about half in the room were introverts, but his advice was to "get over it." Leadership is a people business that cannot be accomplished by e-mail from behind a closed door. "You can be an introvert on your own time." He expected leaders to overcome their preferences and interact.

If Kusy and Holloway are correct about the role of culture in driving toxic leadership, simply removing bad leaders is not enough.[21] Mere removal falls in the category of necessary, but insufficient. Military organizations could find themselves quite busy identifying and removing destructive leaders unless they address the underlying dynamics that spawn and sustain them.

## What If You Are the Toxic Leader?

Those who have an inkling that they might be a toxic leader should probably listen very carefully to that inner voice. Remember that when it comes to leadership it is the perception of the followers, not necessarily the intentions of the leader that matter the most. If your followers believe you are toxic and are having a negative impact on the organization, then congratulations—you have earned the toxic leader badge.

One senior leader had a personal philosophy of leadership that compelled him to never walk past a deficiency. During a visit to an installation away from his headquarters, he engaged in a lengthy—and, quite frankly, boring—presentation. When one of the attendees nodded off, he noticed and shouted from the podium, "You there, wake her up!" He went on to explain that if he was willing to come all the way there to give a speech, the least she could do was stay awake. He was right, and she was wrong, but the manner in which the correction was made, the obvious power differential between them, and the fact that he had shouted at her in public and in front of her peers made it problematic. After the presentation was complete and the dignitary had departed to return to his headquarters, the talk among the audience was less about the substance of his talk and more about what a jerk he was for publicly humiliating a subordinate. Those who had experience with the officer observed that his behavior constituted a pattern over time. Some respected his attention to detail and saw his aggressiveness in taking charge when things were not going well as an asset, but many saw it as boorish behavior. Although he likely intended to model an alert and action-oriented leadership style, he failed to fully consider how others would perceive his disproportionate use of power.

Feedback is the breakfast of champions, and if subordinates are given an opportunity to provide it they will, especially if it is collected in a manner that assures anonymity. The right questions should be asked. Many climate assessments have been oriented to questions of sexual harassment or race relations. While those are important issues worthy of assessment, some questions directed toward identifying problematic leadership are also a good idea. That type of questioning requires some restraint on the part of the leader, who may receive information that is painful or infuriating. Everyone will be watching, so the surest way to ensure that that kind of information does not flow well is to figuratively shoot the messengers. But when subordinates draw up the courage to provide feedback to a superior, they are bestowing a gift. The appropriate response is to be appreciative. It can be demoralizing to subordinates when they provide feedback to a powerful supervisor and it results in no change. There's nothing more effective in fostering cynicism than offering a glimmer of hope for a better day only to have it snatched away by inaction.

In his autobiography former chairman of the Joint Chiefs of Staff and Secretary of State Colin Powell asserted, "Leadership is solving problems. The day soldiers stop bringing you their problems is the day you have stopped leading them. They have either lost confidence that you can help them or concluded that you do not care. Either case is a failure of leadership."[22] Supervisors should be alert to sudden decreases in information flow and be receptive to after-hours phone calls. Just because bad information isn't coming into the boss's office doesn't mean that bad things aren't happening. Encouraging the frank and honest flow of information up and down the chain of command is a full-time job, and behavior of the leader is a key factor in determining whether it happens. Because subordinates want to please their superiors, it is sometimes necessary to be alert to weak signals that there is something amiss.

An overreliance on the chain of command can isolate a leader from what is happening at lower levels of the organization. Wise leaders find ways to circumvent the chain of command without undermining it. Walking around, providing opportunities for casual conversations, skip-level meetings, and dining with the troops are all time-honored ways of collecting information.

Sometimes spouses and family members are good sources of information as well. If their loved ones are suffering they will rarely sit in silence. Leaders need confidants who can tell them what they need to hear. Sometimes trusted members of the personal staff can fulfill that role. Chaplains, the ship's doctor, or a senior enlisted advisor also may be helpful. Friends who have served at similar levels, former supervisors, mentors, and family members can also be useful sources of feedback and support.

A self-assessment checklist could help to identify areas worthy of attention. Consider the following questions in a moment of quiet solitude, and try to be absolutely honest with yourself. It might help to think about how your subordinates would respond. Share the results with someone who knows you well and who will point out areas where your opinion might be different from what others perceive. Indicate the degree to which you agree with the following questions on a scale between never and all the time (never, infrequently, occasionally, more often than not, most of the time, and all of the time).

1. Information coming to me is being filtered or modified based on my reactions.
2. I am spending my time and energy at the level of leadership expected of someone in my position and pay grade.
3. I encourage the expression of loyal dissent.
4. I am tolerant of constructive criticism.
5. I criticize subordinates in front of others.
6. Those I work with are withholding dissenting views in an effort to avoid conflict.
7. I tend to lose my temper in public.
8. I seek feedback from others.
9. I frequently express appreciation for the work of others.
10. I take credit for the work of others.
11. I tend to use sarcasm.
12. I use threats to motivate others.

13. I withhold information from others that they need to do their jobs.
14. I foster competition.
15. I am a good listener.
16. I get ahead at others' expense.
17. I say thank you.
18. When things go wrong I seek to blame someone.
19. I find it difficult to trust others.
20. I am attuned to unit climate.
21. I take time to develop subordinates.
22. I am someone you do not want to cross.
23. I treat subordinates differently based on whether I like them or not.
24. I have a long-term vision for the organization.
25. People in my organization enjoy working here.

After mulling over the responses, determine whether there is something on the checklist that you would like to score higher or lower on. That should help to set an agenda for behavior change.

Once a supervisor is in possession of data that suggest toxicity is a problem, the hard work of behavior change needs to begin. It can be a humbling blow to the ego to receive such disheartening information, but it is important to avoid overreaction. Attempting to radically change one's behavior is an exhausting endeavor that is unlikely to be successful in the long run, but small changes in behavior can have significant impact over time. Besides, there may be aspects of your personality or approach that are key to your success—don't throw the baby out with the bathwater. Instead, focus on increasing composure, being less sarcastic, or increasing relationship-oriented behaviors. Try focusing more effort on developing subordinates and being appreciative of others' contributions. Search less for deficiencies and more for people doing things right. Praise in public and criticize in private. Listen more and speak less. Practice what Judith Umlas calls "grateful leadership."[23] Find ways to acknowledge the good work of others, write appreciative notes, and never miss an opportunity to say thank you. It might feel forced and unnatural at first, but that will pass when the positive impact on subordinates becomes apparent.

Leaders should attempt to foster an environment where others want to give information and feel free to register tactful dissent at the appropriate time and place. A field grade officer used an unusual but effective technique to encourage loyal dissent. He called an enthusiastic subordinate into his office and gave him a directive; when the junior officer turned to leave to accomplish the task, he stopped him. "Wait," he said. "Did what I just told you to do make sense?" The junior officer was confused, shrugged, and said, "You're the boss." "No," said the supervisor, "it is not your job to run out of this office and do stupid stuff that I tell you to do. It is your job to tell me that it is stupid." He then approached the junior officer and said, "Look me in the eye and say, 'Sir, that's bullshit.'" After some encouragement and a few faltering starts, the subordinate managed to do so. "Louder," said the boss. He told the junior officer to ball his fist, pound it on the desk, and proclaim in a loud voice, "Sir, that's bullshit!" The senior officer gleefully joined in: two officers, one senior and one junior, laughing, pounding the desk with their fists, and screaming, "Sir, that's bullshit!" The senior was good to his word, and he never reacted negatively when the junior officer voiced a concern or objection (though the junior officer wisely did not make a habit of pounding his fist on the boss's desk).

A time-honored process for behavior change is to first recognize problematic behavior and envision what success would look like if the change were to come to fruition. Then establish a date on the calendar that marks the point in time when the change will be accomplished. Dates and deadlines make things real while nebulous untethered goals can become unfulfilled wishes or "some days." "Some day I will do this," and "some day I will do that." Some day rarely comes without directed effort. With a clear goal and a deadline for accomplishment, next is to establish some form of accountability mechanism. Accountability mechanisms can include trusted agents, colleagues, mentors, an executive coach, or even subordinates. The important thing is that the accountability mechanism is comfortable providing a clear-eyed assessment of progress toward the goal. Expect it to be difficult at first, with occasional backsliding. Eventually the problematic behavior is likely to recede; then the focus can be shifted to a different behavior. Focus first on the smallest amount of behavior change that will produce the greatest positive benefit.

## Expressing Dissent When Working for a Toxic Leader

To be a good follower, there are circumstances when it will become necessary to confront a powerful supervisor and give voice to disagreement. Such situations are dilemmas in the truest sense of the word: you are faced with a negative outcome in all directions. Sometimes the alternatives are not between good and bad, or right and wrong—the only options will be bad, terrible, awful, and catastrophic. The necessity of speaking truth to power with a toxic boss represents a situation with few pleasant outcomes.[24] It is a situation that requires no small measure of moral courage.

Jim Collins identified five stages of organizational decline: hubris born of success, undisciplined pursuit of more, denial of risk and peril, grasping for salvation, and capitulation to irrelevance or death. Stage three, the denial of risk and peril, can result from an erosion of the healthy group dynamics that foster open dialogue and debate. As General George S. Patton Jr. said, "If everyone is thinking alike, then somebody isn't thinking."[25] In dysfunctional and failing organizations there is a shift to either consensus bordering on groupthink or forms of highly autocratic, even dictatorial, decision making.[26] An ability to tolerate and even encourage loyal dissent is a characteristic of healthy leadership teams. Teams headed by toxic leaders, which can rarely be described as healthy, represent a special case worthy of some exploration. In those organizations even loyal expression of dissent is viewed as an affront to the toxic leader's authority. Toxic leaders have a tendency to view those who are not 100 percent in agreement with them as enemies to be vanquished.

Good followers are not mere sheep or mindless automatons. They should think critically and assert themselves as individuals, committed to complementing their supervisors but also dedicated to the goals of the organization.[27] Occasionally those values come into conflict. Some degree of personal loyalty is virtuous, but Ira Chaleff advocates maintaining a clear focus on the purpose of the organization and its values as a guide for followers.[28] Followers have an obligation to challenge and disobey when lives are being risked unnecessarily, common decency is being violated, laws are sacrificed to expediency, the organization's purpose is undermined, the organization's stakeholders are denied a basic service, and when special interests are being served at the expense of the common good.[29] Military organizations tend to place great value on both personal and organizational loyalty. Julie Irwin suggests that unethical behavior in organizations is frequently driven by misplaced loyalty to a morally compromised "great leader."[30] She argues that "this entire model of the fearless leader and the loyal minions—it relies on a childlike view of leadership that does not benefit anyone."[31]

We should not underestimate the consequences of dissent by courageous followers. Whether they are right or wrong, toxic leaders can be expected to react strongly to even loyal and well-meaning dissent. Followers should therefore be selective in voicing opposition and avoid confrontations over trivial matters. Military personnel are obligated, however, to disobey unlawful orders. Lieutenant Colonel Mark E. Cantrell has provided some sage advice to consider when doubting the wisdom of an order.[32] He recommends exercising caution before jumping to conclusions by taking the time to be quite sure the boss is wrong. It is generally a good idea to assume the supervisor has information that subordinates do not and to give some deference to greater wisdom or a broader perspective. Sometimes the timing and delivery of the message can make a difference. Those in positions of authority sometimes have difficulty admitting mistakes, so it is advisable to argue the point in private before it is announced publicly. Cantrell advocates a tactful, calm, unemotional, but firm approach. Sometimes a written document has more impact than a conversation. His next piece of advice concerns where the line is typically crossed with toxic leaders. If the issue is critically important and efforts to argue the case are unsuccessful, the subordinate should inform the superior that they intend to make the case to the next person in the chain of command. That is an approach that is morally supportable and maybe even necessary, but it is also likely to garner claims of disloyalty and worse from a toxic leader.

Failure to take a stand carries consequences as well, not only for the organization but also for subordinates. Continuous compromise to avoid a reaction from a bad leader is inauthentic and can exact a personal toll. It can be quite demeaning to suppress a deeply held value or belief. Increased anxiety, guilt, loneliness, frustration, burnout and a sense of hypocrisy are often the price to be paid for continued subservience.[33]

Sometimes confrontation works. An aide de camp to a powerful general who had a reputation for being difficult to work for felt that he wasn't doing much right. His boss was very exacting and despite best efforts, whatever the aide did seemed to annoy the general. The aide felt micromanaged and ineffective. After months of struggle he decided to relate his concerns frankly and honestly, no matter the consequences. He resolved that his had been an enjoyable career, but he just could not continue with the status quo. He then outlined, in writing, how much he really wanted to do a good job and how devoted he was to the welfare of the general and the organization. He related several instances of how the general undermined his efforts and the degree to which such behavior negatively impacted him. What he got in return was several weeks of silence. Then one day, while riding in an automobile, the general took out the note and read it aloud, word for word. He then looked up and said, "That took balls." From that point forward their relationship changed significantly for the better.

Apparently the general appreciated the gutsy approach and took seriously his aide's dedication. He became the aide's greatest cheerleader and advocate, and the aide became a trusted and dedicated confidant. The general was still a demanding and difficult boss, but the transformation led to a much healthier working environment. Sometimes supervisors know they are difficult to work for and appreciate a well-timed and appropriately delivered reminder.

When going over the head of a toxic leader do not expect to be appreciated for taking a principled stand. It is best to anticipate that your time in the organization is coming to an end and that this sometimes means the end of a promising career. An enlightened leader once advised his subordinates to keep in their minds at all times the realization that they could leave the military and be just fine selling insurance if necessary. Those who feel they are indispensable to the organization and are called to lofty heights will more easily compromise their integrity in order to get there. In environments where supervisors do not tolerate dissent, perhaps less forthright measures such as leaking information, filing complaints, going public, and skipping the chain of command are justified. If the impact of continued acquiescence is unacceptable, then self-interest cannot be the only consideration.

# 7   Toxic Coworkers

The toxic source of organizational dysfunction is not always the supervisor. Toxic peers and uncivil subordinates can also negatively impact organizational climate. A 2014 study by the Workplace Bullying Institute reported that most bullies tend to be supervisors (56 percent), but 33 percent of the time the abuse comes from peers at the same level of the organization.[1] Those who deceive, manipulate, undermine, and place their personal agendas above the welfare of the unit can wreak organizational havoc. As with toxic leaders, they can increase stress levels and reduce satisfaction, cohesion, and sense of purpose—or in terms of the four Fs, they negatively impact fun, fellowship, and feeling and can inflict emotional and physical harm.

It may take some time for their true colors to emerge, but toxic peers can be the source of problematic cliques or subcultures once they have garnered a following. Some people just seem to bring a black cloud with them and inflict misery upon others. Call them inconsiderate, socially challenged, hostile, discourteous, uncivil, or troubled, but regardless how you describe them they have a disruptive influence on others. Cavaiola and Lavender identified a list of personality disorders that can often be descriptive of toxic coworkers:

- Paranoid: Highly suspicious, distrusting, cold.
- Schizoid: No desire for human closeness. No close friends. Doesn't understand people and their needs.
- Schizotypal: Really odd, even bizarre. Likely to say something like, "The boss yelled at me, but I didn't care. My body kind of left the room." One schizotypal we knew lived in his car.
- Antisocial: No or little sense of morals. Motto is "Do unto others. Then leave."
- Narcissistic: Self-centered and grandiose to the point where he or she can't consider another's point of view. If narcissism is not too bad, they can be highly effective, usually attracted to leadership positions. Their motto is "What have you done for me lately?"
- Histrionic: Dramatic, flamboyant, overemotional, and shallow.
- Borderline: Moody, angry, with highly intense and stormy relationships. Probably the most likely to litigate. Hold on for one wild roller coaster ride!
- Obsessive Compulsive: Overconscientious, picky, obsessed with details and timeliness. Very perfectionistic. Like narcissists, likely to be successful if disorder is not too bad.
- Avoidant: Afraid of taking risks or having a relationship. Corporate wallflowers.
- Dependent: Can't make individual decisions; needs constant reassurance. Good but insecure team player, often loyal to the company. These individuals are often referred to as codependent.
- Passive Aggressive: Angry, but won't show it overtly. Covert expressions of anger include inefficiency, blaming management and other authority figures, tardiness, and other quietly obstructionistic behavior.[2]

As with toxic leaders, toxic peers thrive when others do not intervene. It is understandable why peers might not want to address a toxic coworker head on. If the chain of command that has the power and authority to handle a personnel situation fails to address the situation, why should peers risk taking matters into their own hands? A 2014 study by the Workplace Bullying Institute reported 72 percent of American employers either condoned or explicitly sustained bullying and less than 20 percent took actions to stop it.[3] Without positional power it is natural that peers would seek to avoid the offender rather than attempt to resolve the situation.

Avoidance is a legitimate approach. Don't allow toxic coworkers to suck you into their negative vortex. Do not be quick to respond to perceived insults. Focus instead on your area of responsibility and politely decline to engage or retaliate. Take protective measures to ensure your own well-being. It can be difficult to avoid the fray, but taking the moral high ground can avoid being dragged through the mud. Sometimes avoidance is not possible because of bullying behavior or attacks that cannot be ignored. In such cases, a clear and direct response is called for. In the case of a clear expression of disapproval, toxic colleagues will sometimes back off and look for others to go play their dysfunctional games with.

Harry Dolan, the former Chief of Police of Raleigh, North Carolina, has advocated a "knock it off" approach. He observed that much of the time it is not necessary to resort to formal write-ups, counseling, evaluations, or other official mechanisms when a colleague begins to stray. In fact, resorting to administrative processes can be an overreaction. A simple but emphatic "Hey, knock it off" may be an effective means of establishing that certain behaviors are outside acceptable norms.

In some instances, a group response can be influential. A new company commander queried his first sergeant about the lack of personnel issues that crossed his desk. In his previous unit the young officer had spent quite a bit of time dealing with problem soldiers. In his present unit there were almost no incidents of non-judicial punishment or need of intervention by the commander. The first sergeant explained that the unit had a strong sense of pride. They thought of themselves as elite, and they valued their reputation as an excellent unit. If a soldier failed to perform or acted in a way that brought dishonor upon the unit, fellow soldiers tended to take matters into their own hands by clearly explaining, as a group, that it was unacceptable to screw up their squad. Peer pressure of the positive if somewhat threatening sort was quite effective in most instances. When peer influence wasn't helpful, the chain of command was there to take action, usually with plenty of evidence supplied by other soldiers.

We learn early in life that nobody likes a tattletale, and there is a tendency to keep information that supervisors could use close to the vest until witnesses are compelled to come forth. Frequently peers are hesitant to report the dysfunctional behavior of their colleagues out of a desire to "keep it in the mess" or a sense of loyalty to others of their station. However, the longer it takes to get information to the right authorities, the longer toxic colleagues have to disrupt the climate. Occasionally the toxic peers are clueless about the negative impact of their behavior. Because it takes so long for their colleagues to muster up the courage to address the situation either directly or with the help of supervisors, the offender may assume his or her behavior is acceptable practice in that organization.[4] Also, supervisors may want to address a situation but feel hampered by a lack of evidence. Most leaders prefer to avoid being overruled by an appeal and will therefore take action only when they feel they have a fully justified case. In other words, bad news and lateral abusers do not get better with age.

Leaders can foster an environment where abusive behavior is not tolerated by being alert for subtle indications that there is a problem. The signs can usually be found if they are actively looked for. Trusted advisors, climate surveys, and sensing sessions can sometimes be helpful in diagnosing a problem. If the climate is not already too far down the drain, usually someone will be confident and caring enough to provide information to a leader who is perceived as receptive. It helps when those in positions of authority make clear statements about the importance of maintaining a culture of dignity and respect and make themselves accessible to their subordinates. Reputations often precede those who are toxic, and their arrival in the unit is a good time to address the issue.

For example, rumors and lamentations swirled through a unit weeks before a senior noncommissioned arrived to assume a key position. He had a reputation as a poor team player who tended to treat both peers and subordinates with little regard, and quiet efforts to reassign him elsewhere had been unsuccessful. The day he reported for duty, a field grade officer who was not his immediate supervisor took the initiative and pulled him aside to let him know two things: first, that he had the reputation of being a jerk others did not want to work with, and second, that if rumors about his behavior were true, his career would be ended in short order. He appeared legitimately shocked by the revelation that he was thought of as toxic. The approach of properly putting him on notice was successful. Those who had worked with the noncommissioned officer in previous assignments noted a marked and welcome change in the person they thought they knew.

Supervisors should treat complaints that do come to them seriously and confidentially with an eye to protecting those who report from retaliation.[5] But when toxic peers cannot be avoided and there appears to be no impending intervention by supervisors on the horizon, Robert Bramson recommends a six-step coping strategy:

> (1) Assess the situation. (2) Stop wishing the difficult person were different. (3) Get some distance between you and the difficult behavior. (4) Formulate a coping plan. (5) Implement your plan. And (6) monitor the effectiveness of your coping strategy, modifying it where appropriate.[6]

The process of assessment involves some attempt to examine patterns of behavior to discern whether the person is truly difficult or whether there is some situational impetus for the behavior. It is easy to label someone as toxic or abusive, but it can be both harder and more fruitful to attempt to understand why others act as they do. For example, a unit commander had a habit of precipitously diving deeply into any perceived problem that came to his attention. When members of the staff provided him information about an issue, an inevitable full-scale intervention followed. Even minor deficiencies that were easily correctable by lower levels received his personal attention. Some frustrated members of the staff would hesitate to provide the boss with information for fear it would launch a new program. His behavior was explainable through an examination of the relationship the commander had with his immediate supervisor, a demanding toxic leader who put unrelenting pressure on the commander to be "on top of things."

Bramson's advice to stop wishing the person were different is a process of letting go of a cycle of hope that the person will change that will inevitably be followed by resentment when the hope goes unfulfilled. At some point we have to realize that we really can't control other people; we can only control our own reactions to other people. Gaining distance is the process of breaking the patterns of behavior that activate unhelpful reactions by becoming detached from the difficult person. A coping plan is a method of preventing your own buttons from being pushed by the difficult person and changing the dysfunctional pattern of interaction. The first step in coping is to identify and avoid the triggers that prompt your defensive behavior.

A supervisor who had a reputation for being difficult to work for reacted defensively to any form of perceived dissent. He frequently asked for the opinions of others, but when they were given he would become argumentative. An attentive subordinate learned that instead of telling the boss what he didn't want to hear directly, it was much more effective to simply ask questions such as "Do you think that is really the most effective way to accomplish your objective?" or "What do you think others will perceive if you do that?" If skillful and diligent coping does not work, Bramson recommends getting as much distance from the difficult person as possible.

Remember that no one is under a moral obligation to remain in the vicinity of, to keep working with, or even to keep living with another person whose behavior is demoralizing, severely upsetting, or stress producing. I emphasize this point because I keep finding people for whom it is not obvious at all. They confuse a practical question of costs and benefits with a moral imperative.[7]

Bramson's observation requires some modification when applied to military settings. Soldiers may in fact be legally required to remain in the vicinity of stress-producing colleagues, but they should not stay any longer than they are obligated to. If exit is the only way to get away and preserve your mental and physical health, then take it when you can.

In the book *Snakes in Suits*, Babiak and Hare provide some guidance for handling a "psychopathic" coworker.[8] Psychopaths represent a special case because they can also be dangerous due to their utter disregard for the impact of their actions. Avoidance is a good idea, but it is not always possible. They suggest that it is a bad idea to label a coworker as a psychopath; instead, they recommend focusing on their behavior. "Observe it, document it, and if you are intimidated or feel that you are in danger, bring it to the attention of those in authority or someone you trust."[9] Psychopaths can be master manipulators who are not above taking action to reduce the credibility and reputation of someone they perceive to be a threat. This is one case where anonymous reporting might be appropriate. Do not confront psychopaths directly, and if necessary find an exit. Remember that they can be unpredictable and will do almost anything to advance their interests.

In military organizations, camaraderie, attachment to the unit, and a strong sense of mission compete with the desire to leave an abusive situation. Exit sometimes seems like surrender or appeasement, words the American military has a strong aversion to. Sometimes victims stay for other reasons. Mistreatment that is occasional and alternated with friendly treatment can lead victims to feel kindly toward and even bond with their abusers.[10] It seems a bit paradoxical, but sometimes victims develop close relationships with their aggressors. The term Stockholm syndrome derived from a six-day standoff between police, two hostage takers, and four hostages after a failed bank robbery in Stockholm, Sweden. The hostages bonded with their captors despite the fact that the armed criminals were threatening their lives. Small acts of kindness such as providing a coat to a shivering captive, allowing a claustrophobic hostage outside the vault, and permitting a hostage to call family members resulted in a close relationship where the captives began to fear the police more than the gunmen.[11] The crisis was resolved without serious injury when police introduced teargas into the vault. However, one of the captives later became engaged to one of the criminals, and another founded a legal defense fund in support of their former captors. Conditions that are necessary to induce Stockholm syndrome include a perceived threat at the hands of an abuser, perceived small kindnesses from the abuser to the victim, isolation from perspectives other than the abuser's, and a sense that there is no escape from the situation.[12] The phenomenon has been used to explain all sorts of paradoxical attachments beyond hostage taking, where victims have identified with their abusers after traumatic experiences.

Some other dynamics can be observed in organizations where a peer abuser is present. Because of the Jekyll and Hyde nature of toxic peers, colleagues are never sure which version of the person is going to show up on a given day. With the tendency to walk on eggshells and be hypervigilant of the offenders' moods, one person's attitude begins to control the climate of the larger organization. The crotchety colleague derives some benefit from the arrangement, especially if work assignments are subtly shifted to compensate. In a very negative way the offender has an inordinate amount of control over the organization. Other organizational members end up taking up the slack, preferring additional work to having to deal with the unpredictable and volatile coworker.

The inequity of work distribution in such cases can be a source of additional resentment.

Those who escape an abusive situation, whether through permanent change of station, reassignment, or separation from the armed services, should recognize that they might have some healing to do, both physically and mentally, especially if they suffered acutely. Negative emotions have a tendency to resurface later as fear, anxiety, and even aggressive behavior.[13] Long-term exposure to stress also has physical ramifications. The Workplace Bullying Institute identified the following physical indications of stress-related diseases and health complications from prolonged exposure to bullying: nausea, tremors of the lips, hands, or limbs, lack of coordination, chills, profuse sweating, diarrhea, rapid heartbeat, rapid breathing, elevated blood pressure, chest pains, uncontrollable crying, and headaches.[14] The emotional repercussions may include subsequent difficulty trusting others and a hesitation to reestablish healthy relationships with others. Taking some time to process the experience and make sense of it can be a useful endeavor. Writing about the incident can be a cathartic exercise for many, and the process of simply telling the story to others can be helpful. Do not hesitate to reach out to mental health providers. Those who specialize in anxiety disorders, trauma, and abuse can be particularly helpful.

In his book *Meeting the Ethical Challenges of Leadership*, Craig E. Johnson provided a useful chapter on confronting evil, which included the following advice: "Not only do we need to resist situational influences that can turn us into brutes as followers, but as leaders we should eliminate conditions that promote evil behavior in our subordinates. It is our ethical duty to intervene when we see evil behavior and to reward others who do the same."[15] Johnson also made a case for forgiveness as an act that can break cycles of evil. Cycles of evil are characterized by aggression that leads to retaliation followed by additional aggression. Forgiveness is achieved when the aggrieved party tries to understand the abuser. Forgiving does not have to include condoning the behavior, but those who forgive make a conscious choice to avoid passing it on in a way that can result in empathy and compassion for the offender.[16]

Those who forgive make a conscious choice to stop nurturing the memories of insult that caused their humiliation. The story of Louis Silvie Zamperini's life, recounted in a bestselling book and recent major motion picture,[17] provides a fascinating example. During World War II, after surviving a B-24 bomber crash in the Pacific Ocean followed by a harrowing forty-seven days of drifting in a lifeboat in shark-infested waters, Zamperini was captured and later tortured in a Japanese prisoner of war camp. When he returned home from the war, Zamperini was an angry man who drank heavily and was beset by nightmares. After a religious epiphany, he was able to forgive his captors, and he even visited Japan to meet with some of those who had been the source of his torment. In his autobiography, Zamperini wrote about the power of forgiveness: "I forgave and, even better, understood what forgiveness had done for me. Forgiving myself and others was the story of my life. People called me Lucky Louie, and I knew it was true."[18]

Forgiveness results in the reduction or elimination of negative feelings, which brings health benefits. Forgiveness "facilitates the restoration and maintenance of interpersonal relationships, gives release to both the forgiver and the forgiven from negative affect, and offers the possibility of a new beginning free from the damaging legacy of the past."[19]

# 8 Mitigating Toxic Leadership

> Leaders must encourage their organizations to dance to forms
> of music yet to be heard.
> —Warren G. Bennis

The first step in fixing a problem is realizing that you have one. This book has made a case that while effective leadership is a combat multiplier, toxic leadership is a threat to productivity, health, retention, satisfaction, ethics, commitment, and readiness. There is apparently something worse than an absence of leadership. Some behavior by those in authoritative positions serves as a form of anti-leadership. Toxic leadership also has a far-reaching negative impact, extending well beyond the workplace and the traditional indicators of organization effectiveness into aspects of life that are still being discovered. Service members suffer on the job, and their family members struggle along with them.

Providing a vocabulary facilitates discussion of phenomena and their dynamics, so part of the work of increasing awareness and sensitivity is accomplished by putting a name to the experience. Though other descriptors may be equally or more accurate— abusive supervision, petty tyranny, bullying, destructive or bad leadership—"toxic leadership" is a catchy, compelling term that rightly evokes images of poisonous outcomes. Once understood for what it is, who wants to earn that title?

## Organizational Efforts to Reduce Toxic Leadership

Toxic leaders are a problem at both individual and organizational levels. Dealing with destructive leaders requires individualized responses and the marshaling of effort and resources to address the problem from an organizational level. Harvey Hornstein has suggested that it is insufficient to merely teach subordinates how to cope with toxic bosses.[1] That approach shifts responsibility for dealing with an untenable situation to the victims. To change behavior across an organization change at the system level is also necessary. Part of that change involves a shift in mindset to recognize that it is not just those in leadership positions who matter. Leadership does matter, but there are many potential entry points to affect change in organizations, including personnel and management information systems, climate, culture, incentives, metrics, mission statements, and strategic plans. Alan Goldman asserts, "We must seek both short-range and deep-structure solutions. Mismanagement and failure to accurately and timely identify people problems is in itself a form of toxic leadership. Managerial negligence undetected may contribute to malpractice and company-wide toxicity."[2]

Irving Janus provided the term *groupthink* to describe what happens when teams become more interested in maintaining consensus than getting the right answer.[3] Groupthink is a well-known pathology of group decision making and has been a factor in some notable foreign policy debacles including the botched Bay of Pigs invasion of Cuba. During that ignoble chapter of American history President Kennedy's closest advisors failed to voice their reservations about the feasibility and advisability of launching a CIA-sponsored invasion of Cuba using expatriates and refugees trained in Latin America. Kennedy's team had worked hard together while waging a winning presidential campaign, and key advisors hesitated to bring up difficult questions that might have resulted in them being ostracized from that group.

One of the easiest ways to ensure that self-censorship doesn't take hold in teams is to acknowledge the problem directly. An authoritative member of the group can stand up and say, "We will have no groupthink here. I want an open airing of all concerns and opinions." That simple statement sends a reminder to the group and establishes a psychosocial cue that disagreements will be heard. Similarly, allowing "toxic leadership" to enter into the workplace lexicon is useful: naming the problem and discussing it openly begins the process of reducing its prevalence.

Toxic leaders are organizational chameleons who carefully harness systems of power to further their selfish aims.[4] As a result they stand out as negative examples to their suffering subordinates. They eagerly accept missions, are frequently viewed as hard-charging go-getters, and have little concern for unit climate or the long-term welfare of the people who do the work of their organizations. Toxic leaders tend to be accomplishment oriented and in many cases are very dedicated to their organizations. They are also frequently narcissistic with an inflated sense of self-worth and callous disregard for the welfare of others. Often they can go about their destructive business for extended periods of time without triggering an organizational response. They are typically undone when they commit some infraction or a catastrophe occurs that prompts an investigation, which also happens to uncover the unacceptable command climate. As a measure of progress we might anticipate a time when toxic climates are discovered and dealt with before the tragedies occur. Earlier detection and intervention might help mitigate the negative influence of toxic leaders. Such a proactive approach would mark a significant shift in mindset.

Before a more productive approach can take hold it might be necessary to "unlearn" a few things about military leadership. Nystrom and Starbuck assert that to survive and avoid crises organizations must also unlearn by discovering their inadequacies and discarding them.[5] Organizational learning can be hindered when it becomes unacceptable to challenge old ways of thinking, even when there is evidence they are outmoded. Despite increasing expectations of its leaders, the military has tolerated an excessively wide range of leadership styles, and the recognition that no two individuals lead in exactly the same way has led to an anything-goes attitude. Toxic leaders are tolerated for too long, and they are promoted too high into too many positions of responsibility. As when dealing with cancer, early detection is key, but toxic leadership may not be a problem that can be identified and then eradicated in its entirety. Bad leadership is rather a problem that can be better managed with attention to the dynamics that contribute to its prevalence. Perhaps we give too much deference to those in leadership positions. Maybe some of our archetypes about all-knowing, powerful, and autocratic leaders are misplaced. It could be that an unrelenting emphasis on technical ability and martial skill has overshadowed equally important interpersonal skills and behaviors. A great pilot does not necessarily make a good squadron commander, great engineers do not necessarily lead teams of engineers well, and physical prowess does not necessarily translate to effective leadership. Leadership is an activity practiced in the interpersonal domain.

### Personality Type and Emotional Intelligence

Daniel Goleman popularized the notion of emotional intelligence, suggesting that self-awareness, self-regulation, and an ability to read and understand others can be more important than academic intelligence.[6] It certainly helps to be smart, but we live and operate in social groups. Leadership is not simply about being in charge and making good decisions. It also involves motivating, developing, and even inspiring others. For example, during a field exercise a team of soldiers established an elaborate fighting position at a command post entrance. They continuously improved the position over several days and gradually added embellishments. A visiting field grade officer haughtily observed their efforts and proclaimed that studies had proven that a particular arrangement of concertina wire was more effective in stopping wheeled vehicles.

Apparently he failed to take into account a well-camouflaged .50 caliber machine gun emplacement covering the entry point. The officer might have been correct about the effectiveness of the wire placement, but his manner of delivering advice won frosty reactions from the soldiers, and their surreptitious expressions indicated they were less than motivated by his technical observations. This officer had not only missed an opportunity to recognize the extensive effort that had gone into constructing the position, he also had given them no opportunity to explain the multiple layers of security they had put into place. In his effort to prove himself knowledgeable he failed to listen, not only missing an opportunity to learn but also exhibiting a lack of emotional intelligence.

We tend to value leaders who are composed, steady in times of crisis, emotionally sound, and in control of their moods. That is not to say that leaders are expected to be without emotion, distant and unreachable by others. It simply means that they do not indulge the extremes of emotion in terms of duration and intensity.[7] When they fall prey to rage or other strong emotions, leaders appear neurotic or unstable to their subordinates, attributes that are negatively correlated with perceptions of effective leadership. During an emotional memorial ceremony a brigade-level commander became obviously overwhelmed by the moment. During the eulogy her efforts to maintain military bearing failed, and she had to take a few minutes to regain composure. As the soldiers filed out of the ceremony one was heard to say, "Wow, did you see her cry? She must really care about us."

The goal at the organizational level of analysis is to move the mean of leadership as practiced in military formations a bit closer to the exemplary and farther from the toxic. It would also be beneficial to more quickly detect toxicity and intervene with those who are practicing influence-behaviors that are inconsistent with the values of the armed services. Goldman suggests that performance appraisals should be determined, in part, by team and relationship skills, with relationship skills having the higher priority.[8]

Military personnel systems are top-down and leader-centric. The only opinions that count on fitness and evaluation reports are the perceptions of supervisors who rate their subordinates. Supervisors can be fooled, especially if they have a broad span of control. We should not expect senior raters who comment on over fifty personnel evaluations to know their subordinates well. Those responsible for evaluating a large number of subordinates tend to get spread thin and are frequently challenged to devote sufficient time to properly observing, coaching, and mentoring subordinates. Instead, they resort to a crisis response approach by directing their attention to the largest and fastest approaching problem through a form of organizational firefighting.

Overburdened supervisors also tend to overestimate their ability to discern what is going on in subordinate units and are frequently surprised to find out the extent of suffering that takes place when their direct reports become toxic. Followers know when they are being abused, but aside from the drastic step of filing a formal complaint they have few means of signaling when there is a problem. When an investigation has concluded and the report has documented the full negative impact of a toxic leader, a classic response is shock and dismay that the situation was so bad. Unfortunately the promotion and command selection processes that exclusively rely on top-down assessments are as likely to promote a toxic leader as one who is not toxic. The reaction to the promotion of well-known toxic leader is characteristic: a palpable sense of distress accompanied by a questioning of the organization's collective wisdom. At some point a toxic leader's reputation may come to the attention of someone who sits on a selection board, but that is a matter of chance, not design. Inflated evaluation and fitness reports do a poor job of identifying those with destructive leadership styles. However, toxic leaders can be found if mechanisms are put into place to find them.

Military organizations do have offices that function as safeguards to identify situations requiring intervention beyond the chain of command. In the civil sector the responsibility for hearing and investigating worker complaints typically falls to the human resources office, an entity that has no exact equivalent in military units. Instead, service members can access inspectors general, staff judge advocates, and even chaplains. Those who have the responsibility of serving in the role of institutional watchdog should be especially attuned to indicators of toxic leadership, and they should be receptive and aggressive in its identification and elimination. Those in command who make the ultimate decisions about whether a leader is removed should be equally attentive to complaints of toxic leadership.

## Moving Beyond Supervisor-Centric Evaluations

At some point it is necessary to collect and consider data from subordinates. They should not necessarily be asked to evaluate their supervisors' job performance because they might not have the experience or perspective to understand the roles and responsibilities of their bosses. They can, however, indicate whether they have faith and confidence in their leaders, whether they are being abused, whether they feel their supervisors care about them, and whether they perceive that they are receiving adequate training and guidance. Some are dubious about using subordinate feedback in any formal way out of concern that military leaders might pander to their subordinates and fail to lead aggressively for fear of getting a bad evaluation. That is a legitimate concern, but it also underestimates military personnel. As Powell observed, "American soldiers will gripe constantly about being driven to high performance. They will swear they would rather serve somewhere easier. But at the end of the day they always ask, 'How'd we do?' "[9] Military personnel typically are quite adept at discerning the difference between an easy leader and a good one.

Subordinate data can be obtained by several means, including 360-degree assessments and climate surveys. Multirater assessments, also known as 360-degree instruments, ask individuals to evaluate themselves on established criteria and then compare the self-assessment to the opinions registered by superiors, peers, and subordinates. Such schemes, which provide an opportunity to calibrate one's self-opinions, are a mainstay of professional development programs and executive coaching initiatives. Typically 360-degree instruments are used for developmental purposes, which is to say that the results are provided only to the individuals and not to their supervisors. The assumption is that a leader will be motivated to properly interpret such data and improve as indicated. That is a questionable assumption with toxic leaders, however; they are quick to reject feedback, especially if it comes from subordinates.

To date, military schemes to access 360-degree data have been long on data and short on interpretation, analysis, and intervention. They are typically driven by extensive, elaborately designed information-technology backbones, but they have lacked one-on-one face-to-face feedback from those trained to interpret the data and ensure they are understood. Executive coaching has not caught on widely in the military, but any good coach would say that the instrument used is far less important than the discussion that the process introduces. Many consider the provision of data to clients without an accompanying one-on-one feedback session by a trained and licensed practitioner to be an unethical practice. That does not necessarily mean that those who give feedback must be mental health clinicians, but they should have a thorough understanding of the psychometric instruments they use and be well trained in talking others through the process. They should also be alert to when it is appropriate to refer to mental health practitioners.

Military organizations might be well served by adopting the services of good executive coaches. Some commands have experimented with the use of coaches for key positions, especially in the navy, but reliance continues to rest mostly on the chain of command for everything from mentoring, to coaching, to evaluation. Many in uniform believe that the only people who can provide useful advice to them are those who have served at or above their level, but there is no evidence that is that case. At least one thirty-year-old executive coach with no military experience has successfully coached a number of navy flag officers. A study in 2009 assessed the extent to which lieutenant colonels and colonels had access to multirater feedback. A sample of war college students found that among the 37.4 percent of respondents who had received 360-degree feedback at some point during their careers, 59.3 percent felt it was effective.[10] If the army data generalize to the larger force, there is work to be done in both the penetration and effectiveness of multirater processes.

The army has long had a process in place for peer evaluations among flag officers. That process provides senior officers with the opportunity to weigh in with their perceptions of their contemporaries. As currently configured the process does not include subordinate data but does provide an additional data point for consideration, which is beneficial precisely because it exists outside the typical top-down evaluation process. The chairman of the joint chiefs of staff, General Martin Dempsey, is reportedly expanding the peer evaluation program to all generals and admirals.[11] If it works well for general officers it might be useful for other ranks as well, but a top-down implementation schedule is most appropriate when searching for toxic leaders.

There is a penchant in the military to solve personnel issues from the bottom up, starting with junior enlisted soldiers and junior officers who represent the future of the organization. Early socialization is important, and for that reason discussions of leadership style and destructive leadership should be incorporated into the early stages of professional military education. Prevailing wisdom holds it can be hard to teach old dogs new tricks, but senior staff members are role models who have remarkable reach by virtue of their example. For example, a division commander once publicly remarked that his favorite alcoholic beverage was a particular brand of high-end bourbon; to his amazement that brand of alcohol soon became the top seller at the post's liquor store. In a similar way the leadership style and preferences of high-ranking officers will be noted and emulated. Senior personnel might not have as long of a period remaining in uniform, but they have the power and position to do great harm, and they also serve as a powerful example of what organizational success looks like.

Unit climate surveys are another means of providing information about the health and welfare of military units. They have been used in various ways in the armed forces, and have often been focused on sexual harassment and race relations. Equal opportunity and gender dynamics are important, but the quality of leadership in an organization is also worthy of analysis. Climate surveys can be less threatening than 360-degree feedback because they are not focused on any one individual. They also typically require fewer resources to implement and are more widespread in use. The war college study found that 70 percent of respondents had participated in a climate study, of whom 46.7 percent felt it was effective.[12] Those statistics suggest that climate studies have received greater penetration than multirater tools with a lower level of satisfaction with their effectiveness.

One reason why such surveys might be less than fully effective has to do with where the data end up. If climate data are only provided to a commander who is a large part of the problem, little is accomplished. Climate data should be systematically collected and analyzed to find and intervene with units that are several standard deviations off the mean. Climate surveys also depend on the honesty of those completing the questionnaires. If the unit climate lacks trust or has widespread fear of retribution, the results of a survey may not be reliable. Respondents can be expected to reply honestly only if they are assured of anonymity.

If unit members take the risk of participating in a survey process to no good effect, they will be less likely to answer frankly in the future. For example, problems with the leader of an army unit eventually came to the notice of his superiors. Although no official complaints had been filed, the general sense of low morale and dissatisfaction in the leader's unit was telling. In this case a skilled and experienced psychologist initiated a 360-degree process along with a one-on-one feedback session. The subordinates who were asked to complete the evaluation discussed among themselves whether they should respond forthrightly to the survey. Some felt it too risky to be completely honest, so they tempered their criticism but did point out areas for improvement. Hopes were high that the process might have some positive effect on the supervisor, but months after the 360-degree instrument had been completed there was no observable change in his behavior. Perhaps the struggling supervisor was not sufficiently motivated to change, or had dismissed the entire process, or was incapable of acting on the feedback. In that case, the unit members would have been better off had they not known about the intervention as the result was a form of organizational letdown and an increasing sense of futility.

## The Importance of Interpersonal Skill

It might be helpful to develop and select for leadership positions not simply on the basis of short-term effectiveness but also with an eye to leadership style. There are many who get the job done, but who gets the job done while taking good care of the team? Retired Lieutenant General Walter F. Ulmer Jr., former III Corps commander and former CEO of the Center for Creative Leadership, suggests that we visualize military units as large human batteries. They have a finite amount of energy available to do work at a given point in time, and much of the available energy is taken up accomplishing routine tasks—just getting through the day. Units can be prompted to operate at a high level of intensity for a limited period of time, but eventually the available energy gets depleted. Good leaders recharge the organization, sparking higher levels of commitment, creativity, and enthusiasm. Others, merely by virtue of their interpersonal style, drain the unit's energy. Such demanding leaders have sometimes been referred to as human "sweat grenades" because when they enter the room everyone bursts into a sweat.

Some leaders are so destructive they are actually an impediment to mission accomplishment. Work gets done in spite of them not because of them, and subordinates go under, over, or around them to accomplish the mission. They are the ones who require expeditious identification and elimination. Ulmer agreed with a bold and succinct recommendation from a 2010 study of army division commanders:

> "Revise significantly the process for selection to O-6 [colonel] command to ensure that there are no future candidates for Division Command who have been identified clearly as toxic leaders. Specifically, provide boards selecting brigade-level commanders with supplemental data summarizing leadership behavior assessments taken from a sample of officers who had served as company commanders or principal staff offices when the individuals being considered were their battalion commanders." The description of a proposed pilot study of this procedure explains that the assessments of subordinates are taken usually one to three years after the candidate for O-6 command has departed the previous battalion-level command.[13]

Ulmer is essentially recommending adoption of Robert Sutton's "no asshole rule,"[14] a zero-tolerance policy to ensure that no toxic leaders are advanced to division-level command or beyond. Division command is certainly a key position for which special attention is warranted, but we might ask why stop there? Some of the most notorious toxic leaders exist in branches that do not typically qualify for division command, and they can wreak havoc on their organizations.

Organizational metrics should include indicators of long-term health and wellness of unit members as well as short-term measures of success. The G-1 (personnel officer) of an airborne infantry division once provided some good advice to incoming company commanders and first sergeants at a precommand course. Such courses are common in the military for those who are about to assume key positions, to acquaint them with the priorities unique to particular times and locations and to punctuate the importance of their impending role. The G-1 recognized that the commanders were an ambitious and energetic lot, all keyed up for their shot at leading some of the finest soldiers in the world. He acknowledged that they would likely be in command for only one year, two at the most, and that they probably had already amassed a long list of things they hoped to accomplish in that time period. For them it was a sprint to put their mark on the famed division in the limited amount of time available to them, but he asked them to consider the soldiers and noncommissioned officers who were there before they arrived and would remain long after they departed. Those soldiers had already seen a progression of hard-charging company commanders and first sergeants. For them the division was a career, not a command tour, and they could not sprint for twenty years or more. His advice for the new leaders was to consider the impact of their ambitions and temper them for the sake of the long run.

It is not enough to focus solely on the positive aspects of good leadership with lists of traits and competencies. The military services have done a fine job of describing what good leadership is supposed to look like; the bar is appropriately set quite high, and as a result military personnel expect to be led well. So spending time and resources on examining how leadership is actually practiced would be appropriate. It should not be taboo to discuss and learn from examples of bad leadership—the negative examples are out there, and much can be learned from them. All services would benefit from implementing the kind of annual leadership assessment conducted by the Center for Army Leadership, and an assessment across the services by the Department of Defense would be useful as well.

Implementing tools and processes to identify toxic leaders is an important step, but dealing with them once they are identified is an equally important and challenging task. Some leaders at the more toxic ends of the spectrum are not salvageable, and they should be moved out of positions of responsibility and trust without delay to cut the organization's losses and make room for those who lead well. Thomas Ricks noted that the military has not always been so hesitant to remove officers from command. During World War II officers, even generals, were removed when they did not work out, and they were frequently given another chance in a different job.[15] Others might be worth additional investment through behavior modification, retraining, coaching, and careful monitoring.

Most military organizations place inordinate emphasis on the chain of command, expecting raters to evaluate subordinates and to coach, advise, and mentor them as well. A strong chain of command is of benefit, but it also brings challenges. Information sometimes flows up and down the chain of command slowly, if at all, and leadership style is a key variable in determining whether frank and honest information flows easily. Subordinates can be hesitant to present bad news to a volatile boss, so those who react poorly to bad news are less likely to receive it in a timely manner. The chain of command also serves as a natural filter for information. Lower levels wish to demonstrate that they can handle things without unwanted "help" from above; the result is a slight shading of information as it passes up the organizational chain, not because subordinates are intentionally attempting to mislead but merely because they want to please the boss. So here is a warning to senior-level commanders: if your PowerPoint slides are perfectly formatted, without discernible errors, and your briefings are well orchestrated, presented with the skill of an evening major network newscast, your information is probably being overly processed. A remedy is to take some meals with the troops and find opportunities to engage in casual conversation with those several levels down. Cultivate and protect those who give it to you straight, and keep an eye on your gatekeepers and close associates who might, in an attempt to be helpful, be overcontrolling your access or protecting you from bad news.

Evaluators in the rating chain do not necessarily make good coaches, advisors, or mentors. The process of evaluation tends to trump other beneficial developmental activities. Many junior officers report that they aren't being mentored.[16] Colonel Peter

Varljen recommended that the army do away with the term "mentor" altogether and simply focus on educating leaders on how to develop their subordinates through effective coaching, counseling, and role-modeling.[17] The corporate sector has discovered it is often better to hire executive coaches from outside the rating chain and frequently from outside the organization altogether.

A cottage industry seems to have grown up around the promise of increasing emotional intelligence in organizations. The argument for enterprise-level interventions to raise emotional intelligence as a counter to narcissism and toxic leadership goes something like this: if the organizations of leaders who are emotionally intelligent tend to have better command climates, then some level of investment in increasing the prevalence of emotional intelligence is a good idea. However, caution is advisable when using broad-brush training schemes to develop emotional intelligence. Evidence for the success of organization-level initiatives to increase the general level emotional intelligence is lacking.[18] They can be useful in heightening awareness and building collective resolve, but it is not likely they will significantly impact toxic leaders. Highly tailored interventions at the individual level may have some positive impact if a toxic leader is properly motivated by a perceived need to grow and learn. With this in mind, the best approach to deal with toxic leaders probably rests with identification and referral to individualized interventions combined with a very clear understanding that their future in the organization depends on their ability to change their ways.

At the heart of any successful intervention is a willingness to have hard discussions. Most supervisors would understandably rather avoid confronting toxic leaders, especially if they are otherwise getting the job done. Conflict avoidance, however, benefits only the toxic leader. The idea of having hard discussions came up after a presentation on toxic leadership to a midsized corporation. The entire senior leadership team of the company was present in the room, including the president and CEO, a fine gentleman who was very interested in leader development. He had invested significant time and resources into preparing his team for the next level, and they had benefitted from fast growth, capable operations, and a good reputation in the industry. After the case had been made for toxic leadership's negative impact, the audience was obviously restless. Something was going on in the room; a low murmur rose, notes were passed, and eye contact was shifting rapidly around the room. Concerned that he had lost the audience the speaker stopped the presentation and acknowledged that something was amiss. The president and CEO then disclosed what was actually going on: the leadership team had been suffering at the hands of two toxic leaders for some time, and everyone on the team knew who the offenders were. "You have not only convinced us," said the CEO, "but you have given us permission to address the problem. Would you mind stepping into the hallway for bit? We are about to have a hard discussion." Good for them—they were willing to engage in the hard and uncomfortable task of addressing the presence of toxic leadership in their midst.

In an *Army Times* interview in 2000, before the intensive deployment cycle that followed the U.S. response to the 9/11 attacks, General John Keane, then vice chief of staff of the army, observed that the "quality of leadership—as reflected in the mentoring process—has fallen off." He asserted, "We're just not taking the time that we need to spend with our youngsters and their personal growth and development. We need to do more of that."[19] Since then the armed forces and especially the army and marine corps have endured more than a decade of protracted conflict, which has undoubtedly stressed the force. The impact of multiple combat deployments on men, women, and equipment has been apparent. It is a testimony to the dedication and resilience of the armed services that the force is in as good a shape as it is, still ready and able to do the bidding of America's people, as directed by its civilian masters.

As Ulmer put it, "Our institution is by no means broken, but it deserves some refurbishing."[20] After every major conflict the armed forces enter a period of intense renewal, reflection, and recovery, during an inevitable drawdown that shifts money and personnel away from the Department of Defense. In previous postdrawdown periods a group of stewards of the profession stepped forward with an eye to the future and conflicts unfathomed. Renewing the force physically, mentally, and ethically might well be the great work of the next generation of military leaders. As part of that process a continued focus on good leadership, not only as an aspiration but also in practice, would be a worthy investment. Ensuring that soldiers, sailors, airmen, and marines are led in the manner they deserve is not only a means to a better fighting force it is also the right thing to do.

# Conclusion

> Leadership is simply the ability of an individual to coalesce
> the efforts of other individuals toward achieving common
> goals. It boils down to looking after your people and ensur-
> ing that, from top to bottom, everyone feels part of the team.
> —Frederick W. Smith

The misperception that any leadership approach that results in mission accomplishment is a good one is a central problem with many contemporary conceptions of military leadership. Just getting the job done fails to account for a host of important factors, including ethical considerations. An example from science fiction serves to illustrate the point. The novel *Ender's Game* by Orson Scott Card captured the attention of the army's Training and Doctrine Command because of its depiction of the extensive use of immersive scenarios and simulations.[1] The book tells the story of a young Ender Wiggin, who demonstrates potential as a leader in a war between humanity and an intelligent race of interstellar insects. Ender and others are tested to their limits in a series of increasingly difficult simulations. During their "graduation" exercise Ender's team directs an epic battle that culminates in the utter destruction of the alien species. It is at that point Ender is informed that the graduation simulation was an actual battle. In the feature-length movie based on the book it dawns on Ender that he has become an unwitting but essential participant in genocide. Horrified at what he has done, he becomes inconsolable. In one of the final scenes of the film, when Ender's superior emphatically points out that Ender won, Ender asserts with equal vigor that it is also important to consider *how* one wins.[2]

Getting the job done is the essence of effective military leadership, but it is also important to consider how the job gets done and specifically whether the organization and its people are in position at the end of any given mission to continue with the inevitable next task. The long-term health and welfare of people ought to be of concern to military leaders in a force that consists of recruited professionals. Perhaps it is less of a concern in a largely conscripted army where citizens are compelled to serve, are rapidly trained, and are replaced relatively quickly, but that has not been the case for the American military since President Richard Nixon ended the draft in 1973. Despite the increasing sophistication of the weaponry of war, the military is ultimately only as good as its people.

Leadership styles can and do vary, and though there are many ways to be right when influencing others, there are also a few ways to be wrong. Much of this book has been devoted to making the case that some people in positions of authority treat their subordinates in a manner that is detrimental to long-term organizational effectiveness because it runs counter to the espoused values of the military services. Those who disregard the welfare of their subordinates by engaging in an interpersonal style that results in a poor climate represent not only a localized, individual problem but also a problem for the larger organization. If they are perceived as getting ahead at the expense of their subordinates, the negative impact on organizational members is magnified. By contrast, when personnel perceive that an authority figure is selfless and seeks the attainment of legitimate organizational goals, they are more likely to accept, even if begrudgingly, a rough interpersonal style.

The field of research that examines bad leadership is still emerging, but it has become increasingly apparent that this type of leader has a negative impact on many aspects of organizational life. In the military, much of the argument for reducing the number of toxic leaders has been utilitarian in nature. Bad leadership ultimately results in a less effective fighting force. Those who rule by fear and intimidation might obtain compliance in the short term, but they are less likely to foster commitment in the long term. Therefore, it is appropriate to take action to reduce the number of toxic leaders and mitigate their negative effects. The numerous studies and examples throughout this book have demonstrated the pernicious effects of toxic leadership. Decreases in satisfaction, commitment, cohesion, and inclination to remain in service as well as poor productivity, physical and mental health, organizational citizenship behavior, and even ethical conduct are associated with toxic leadership, as are increases in alcohol consumption and absenteeism. The impact of toxic leadership also can extend beyond the workplace to affect the service members' families and loved ones, who frequently are already under significant stress.

The destructive wake of toxic leaders might extend far beyond what we currently understand. Anthropologist David Matsuda has suggested that toxic leadership can be a factor in suicides.[3] Additional research clearly is necessary, but the anecdotal accounts continue to accrue. A recent report in the *Stars and Stripes* asserted that a sailor's suicide on a naval destroyer resulted in part from "a toxic command climate that involved bullying and retribution."[4] The initial investigation of the sailor's death soon was extended to the leadership climate, which involved abusive supervision by senior enlisted personnel. "The report also found that chief petty officers would hold 'informal' and unauthorized disciplinary reviews and that sailors were not comfortable going to their chiefs with problems because they feared retribution."[5] The navy's investigation noted that the supervisors' failure to intervene in the noncommissioned officers' treatment of subordinates had prompted a second suicide attempt as well. In addition, the investigation uncovered an allegation of sexual assault after an evening of excessive alcohol consumption, representing an extreme betrayal of trust. An admiral who endorsed the report commented,

"I am incredibly disappointed in the leadership triad for allowing a climate of fear and intimidation to take hold and for failing to hold individuals accountable."[6]

Why must service members have to die before attention is given to destructive leadership? Most leadership in military formations is good, but that is not an excuse to turn a blind eye to the abusive, destructive, and toxic uses of power and authority.

Every person in an authoritative position can be perceived as sitting on a spectrum, with exceptional, uplifting influence-behavior at one end and reprehensible, destructive behavior at the other. A few genius leaders have a gift for positively influencing, motivating, and inspiring others, but at the other end of the spectrum are leaders who are exceptionally bad, including those who abuse their positions of authority for personal gain or engage in harassment or sexual assault. Between the two extremes sits everyone else, with most falling in the generally good category. The fact that there is more good overall leadership in the military makes the bad leaders stand out in high contrast. As a result of the almost universally positive depictions of leadership in military rhetoric and publications, expectations of military leaders tend to run high. When service members come to expect good leadership, a sense of disappointment and even betrayal can follow when they do not receive it.

Military organizations are characteristically goal oriented, rational, and pragmatic, so the arguments in this book have focused largely on the negative impact of toxic leaders on organizational climate and effectiveness. However, fundamental moral principles about how individuals ought to be treated are worthy of consideration as well. There are reasons to treat subordinates with respect and dignity outside of the positive outcomes that such behavior engenders. In many Western countries military service takes place in the context of democratic variants of government that hold sacrosanct the rights of individuals, including life, liberty, and the pursuit of happiness. Individuals are important and have intrinsic value, and democratic societies do not willfully trample the interests of their citizens without good cause. Democracies sometimes restrain the will of the majority when the rights of a minority are threatened. The judiciary frequently acts to override the will of the majority in the process of protecting small and less politically powerful groups of people in the name of principles outlined in the constitution.

German philosopher Immanuel Kant suggested that we should never treat others merely as a means to an end, but always as an end in and of themselves.[7] Influence-behavior that is demeaning, belittling, humiliating, and abusive might be successful in the short term under some circumstances, but such behavior runs afoul of principles that affirm the fundamental dignity of others. At a broader level the tenets of most religious faiths have at their essence a call to respect the fundamental dignity of humanity, not only for beneficial societal outcomes but also as an ethical principle to live by, inherently right on its own without need of further justification. In a religious sense concern for the welfare of others reflects a fundamental respect for creation. In an ethical sense the grounds of principle alone make abusing others wrong, regardless of the outcome.

Those who use positions of authority to prey upon their subordinates have an inordinate negative impact on individuals and institutions. Unfortunately, toxic leadership remains a fairly common experience in many organizations, including the military. Additional studies are necessary to discern whether there are differences in the rate of toxic leadership between military and other types of organizations. There is no consensus on just how much bad leadership there has to be to warrant an organizational intervention. It would be hard to argue against an agenda that seeks to increase the number of good leaders while reducing the number of bad ones.

Statements from key officials, including the chairman of the joint chiefs of staff, General Martin Dempsey, reflect an increasing recognition that toxic leaders are a problem for the military.[8] A skeptic might suggest that such acknowledgments are more of a response to widely publicized incidents of senior officer misconduct than a shift in mindset, but the initiative to include more 360-degree reviews of general officers provides tangible evidence that some changes are under way. The Center of Army Leadership's effort to derive annual quantitative data about the quality of leadership as experienced by soldiers and members of the civilian workforce is a commendable approach worthy of emulation by other services and the Department of Defense as a whole. The Department of Defense has conducted large-sample surveys of military organizations in the past to assess phenomena of interest. One salient example is the Armed Forces Equal Opportunity Survey, which assessed the extent to which members of the military and their families experienced racial and ethnic forms of harassment and discrimination.[9] That effort obtained survey responses from 76,754 service members in order to obtain a Department of Defense–wide perspective. A similar type of project would be useful in determining the quality of leadership across the armed services.

Other useful data points that could be of use in identifying the scope of the problem include climate surveys and multifaceted evaluation and feedback mechanisms that collect data beyond the perspective of superiors alone. Of course those tools need to be developed, administered, and interpreted properly. Even a well-crafted survey cannot be relied upon if it is administered in an environment where respondents do not answer truthfully because of fear, pervasive cynicism, and lack of trust. Because toxic leaders are not as apparent to their supervisors as they are to their subordinates, a supervisor-centric evaluation process is insufficient to identify destructive leaders as it is sure to underestimate the scope of the problem. Those in authoritative positions who engage in high levels of control and directive behavior tend to be viewed favorably by their supervisors and are resented by subordinates.[10]

Perceptions by senior officials that toxic leaders are less prevalent today than in the past could be more the result of their view from the top of the hierarchy than an accurate organizational assessment. To derive a clear picture of the problem the right questions need to be asked of the right people, and data collection over time is necessary to determine whether there are any trends. Longitudinal studies using consistent measures are necessary to determine whether any changes have occurred in the quality of leadership over time.

The research completed to date provided some indications of the scope, nature, and impact of the problem. An increasing number of authors are providing useful insights and ways of thinking about good and bad leadership. Our understanding of leadership as a social phenomenon has fortunately extended beyond the study of great men and lists of traits and characteristics to include perspectives that see leadership as an influence process involving both leaders and followers. Scholarship on toxic leadership and related constructs has been especially useful in providing a vocabulary that facilitates helpful discussions about the topic, even if definitions of toxic leadership continue to vary. Understanding is an important first step, but the resolve to address the problem of toxic leadership is likely to follow only when the stewards of the profession muster the will to intervene and reduce tolerance for the use of destructive leadership styles and address the systems and processes that drive toxic cultures.

Those who find themselves in the unfortunate position of working for a toxic leader are admittedly in a rough spot. Relationship-oriented behaviors can serve as a stress reducer when the pressure is on, but such behavior is notably absent with toxic leaders. In a *Psychology Today* article Ronald Riggio identified four ways a supervisor can ruin the career of a subordinate: tarnishing reputations through rumors, bad evaluations, or recommendations; contaminating the subordinates' reputations by associating them with the boss's unethical behavior; being uninterested in and neglecting subordinates' development, thus limiting their career advancement; and being wellsprings of demoralizing negativity that can stunt subordinates' aspirations for career progression.[11] Because toxic leaders are characteristically insensitive to the needs and concerns of subordinates, some circumspection about the ability to cure from below is warranted. Nevertheless, it is the obligation of followers to try to influence their leaders toward more effective behavior and to do what they can to craft a good unit climate. Tact and diplomacy are valuable skills when dealing with a toxic leader because direct confrontation can be a risky process, especially if narcissism is involved and the supervisor feels threatened. Those who courageously provide frank and honest information to superiors perform a valuable if underappreciated service.

Those who are in the unenviable position of working for a bully boss should clearly understand that they are not alone. Conveying that message is a primary reason for this exploration. If some of the approaches contained in this book provide ideas helpful in surviving a toxic leader then it will have served a useful purpose. The good news is that toxic leaders tend to be very responsive to their supervisors and can often be influenced from above. That provides an avenue of potential intervention and hope. Those in positions of authority should look carefully for toxic tendencies in their subordinates and intervene with clear and direct expectations about acceptable and unacceptable behavior. Efforts to increase self-awareness are frequently a good investment, but merely providing data from assessment tools and instruments without one-on-one feedback and coaching is seldom effective. The assumption that a leader will modify their behavior when confronted with data that their leadership efforts are not received well by followers is questionable at best—some leaders might, but that is not behavior typically associated with toxic leaders. Those with narcissistic tendencies in particular are quite good at rationalizing their actions and dismissing the opinions of those who are lower in the organizational hierarchy.

Just as strong metal is forged by heat and hammering, working for a toxic leader can be a developmental, if painful, opportunity. After the pain has faded with the march of time and wounds have healed to become scars, those who have survived toxic environments often look back upon the experience as a formative rite of passage. The experience of working for a bully can provide a sense of perspective and foster an appreciation of good leadership. It also tends to build interpersonal calluses and provides an example of what not to do once the subordinate has attained a position of authority. There is much that can be learned from negative examples, though sometimes learning comes at great cost. Unfortunately, the lesson some subordinates derive is that toxic behavior is a successful approach to advancement and success; when that happens, toxicity can become part of the underlying pattern of assumptions and beliefs of the organization. Once destructive leadership becomes accepted and rewarded, organizational members tend to pass those lessons to new members, resulting in the entrenchment of a toxic culture that can be difficult to change.

If toxic leadership is a product of organizational culture, systems and processes, merely detecting and eliminating those who use destructive styles from positions of influence will not alone rectify the problem.[12] This approach might be a good start for some of the more egregious cases and would provide welcome relief to those suffering under the supervision of toxic supervisor; however, if there are aspects of military culture that contribute to the production and perpetuation of toxic leadership, a deeper dive is required. It is certainly not enough to continuously extol the virtues of good leadership without taking into account that there are influence-behaviors exercised in the name of leadership that are not only unproductive but ethically unconscionable. Some in positions of authority not only fail to add value to their organizations but are a detriment to mission accomplishment merely by virtue of how they treat others. When the leader is bad, additional pressure is put on subordinates to achieve despite the boss. When stress increases, an already difficult job becomes even more so. Developing better means of detecting and dealing with bad leaders is a step in the right direction, but discerning why there are so many in an otherwise world-class organization and why the personnel evaluation processes do not screen them out more effectively is also important work.

Toxic leadership is prevalent where it is tolerated. The military services would benefit from narrowing the current wide band of tolerance for varying leadership styles in favor of rejecting toxic leadership behavior. Focused interventions by trained professionals (clinical psychiatrists and executive coaches) would be a valuable addition to the current supervisor-centric approach. In some cases interventions will involve difficult face-to-face discussions about acceptable and unacceptable influence-behaviors. It may not be possible to fix abusers or change their personalities, but it is possible to change their behavior; if that fails, toxic leaders can and should be removed from positions of authority. Not everyone who enters military service is well suited for the interpersonally demanding and emotionally taxing process of leading others.

Supervisors of toxic leaders often experience a pull between two values. On the one hand they want to be fair and empower their subordinates to lead. They recognize that leadership is not always a popular endeavor. More than most, supervisors recognize that leadership is a demanding and often unappreciated activity. On the other hand they are responsible for the actions of their subordinates and are obligated to intervene when a leader harms the organization or loses the faith and confidence of followers. Removing someone from a key leadership position is not a casual matter. Even toxic leaders deserve due process and a chance to address their weaknesses. Removal for cause has lasting career consequences. Those who consider removing a subordinate because of a destructive leadership style need information they can rely upon, and such information might not be forthcoming in an environment of fear and intimidation, especially when the unit is otherwise its accomplishing assigned tasks.

There are some difficult and complicated questions to consider about whether toxic leadership is being created and tolerated by existing attitudes, cultures, and processes, but exploration of those questions has the potential to identify root causes and make a real and lasting difference. Taking that kind of unvarnished introspective look at an organization requires that organizational members question existing processes, beliefs, norms, and assumptions in a climate of robust inquiry and unrelenting candor. Creating such a climate in a proud, hierarchical, and stratified organization is not always an easy thing to accomplish. If the military cannot accomplish that internally, it must fall to external constituents such as congress, academia, or think tanks to spur the discussion. The U.S. military is entering a phase after a prolonged period of conflict and high operational tempo where such reflection is both possible and necessary. Postwar periods have historically been opportunities for rebuilding and reform, when visionary leaders and deep thinkers focus on great questions that position their organizations for decades to come. Such periods bring unique leadership challenges. It is arguable that motivating military personnel during periods of reduced resources requires exemplary leadership skills. It may well be that the great work of the current generation of military leaders will be to rebuild, repair, and posture the force for threats as yet unseen and unknowable.

Former West Point professor Don Snider has been ardent in questioning whether the army is a profession or merely an obedient bureaucracy.[13] This is a very good question for all branches of the service to consider because military organizations have both bureaucratic and professional tendencies. Militaries are structured in bureaucratic fashion, yet their sense of professionalism serves to counter some of the more dysfunctional aspects of large bureaucracies. Petty tyranny, turf protection, and destructive leadership might be par for the course in a bureaucratic hierarchy, but they are inconsistent with a profession that seeks to serve its client well. Sociologist James Q. Wilson has described the army at war as a craft organization.[14] The daily work of the soldiers in a dispersed operational area is not subject to direct observation, but at the end of the day success or failure is determined based on survival. There is little question about what works and what doesn't—the actions of the enemy make the point rather dramatically, and poor doctrine and faulty equipment are quickly identified. Wilson describes a peacetime army as a procedural organization. Absent the ultimate test of effectiveness in combat, the daily work of soldiers is closely observed for compliance with rules, operating procedures, and military doctrine. Training that is observable substitutes for the real test that comes only during combat. The increased supervision and focus on rules and procedures that occurs during peace can displace the sense of ethos and professionalism necessary to drive high performance during war.

Leadership in general, and leading in the military in particular, is a difficult, demanding, and frequently dangerous business, and not every leader who angers or upsets a subordinate is toxic. It also would be a mistake to interpret the call for a reduction in the amount of toxic leadership as some kind of movement toward a politically correct, "nice" kind of leadership where no voices are raised and no feelings are hurt. Focusing on this topic should not contribute to a timid or unengaged form of leadership where those in positions of authority become afraid to intervene and call out substandard performance for fear of upsetting subordinates. Attempting to make everyone happy in a high-reliability organization is a rookie leadership mistake; those who need to be liked and as a result attempt to pander to their subordinates frequently do not garner respect.

Sometimes addressing substandard performance and compelling others to do things that they would prefer not to do is unpopular, but good leadership does not stem from attempting to please everyone all the time. This does not excuse the demeaning and belittling behavior that is characteristic of abusive supervision. Such behavior is poor form at best, and toxic to trust and commitment at worst. The appropriate leadership style for a given situation is the one that meets the needs of followers and the demands of a given situation. Sometimes the best approach is a hug; at other times the right answer is a firm push. Knowing the difference requires sufficient emotional intelligence to discern the appropriate approach for a given person and situation. The ability to diagnose and intervene with the appropriate behavior at the appropriate time is a large part of the art of leadership, and a substantial amount of self-awareness, self-regulation, and adaptability is equally a large part of its effective practice.

During one presentation on toxic leadership, a chief executive officer, who happened to be a military veteran, commented that he felt a discussion of leadership style had empowered him to deal with the members of his senior management team who were not leading in a manner consistent with the underlying values of his organization. He sensed that a small number of his direct reports were making life much harder than it had to be, not only for their subordinates but also for their peers. Although they were effective enough in terms of profit and loss, they weren't treating others with sufficient dignity and respect. Morale wasn't what it should be, and relationships were often strained. The place just wasn't as fun as it used to be, an observation he previously chalked up to increased stresses from high workload. Several good performers had left the company, but he wasn't certain whether they left because of mistreatment or because they had found better opportunities. Some level of turnover was to be expected after all, but he suspected that the interpersonal style of the managers had been negatively impacting the quality of life of some good people. To the CEO's credit was his discomfort with the situation; but he did not relish a confrontation, even though deep down he knew that something ought to be done. He also hesitated to directly confront them because they performed critical functions for the company, so he did not want to alienate them. However, after being exposed to some of the research on toxic leadership and the costs associated with abusive supervision, he resolved to address their behavior for the greater good. When he did confront the managers, it was not a comfortable conversation, but it did make a difference in their workplace behavior. It also sent a message throughout the organization about what he valued and the importance he placed on attracting and retaining talented people. The subordinates of managers with toxic tendencies noticed the difference and appreciated the CEO's intervention.

Sometimes we just need a bit of encouragement to address the issue. If any readers have suspicions about the leadership style of their subordinates and are in search of permission to intervene, consider this permission granted. As the above vignette demonstrates, toxic leadership is not a phenomenon that is in any way limited to the military. There may be some aspects of military organizations that make them prone to destructive leadership, but there is no evidence that the fundamental dynamics of the relationship between a toxic leader and subordinates, or the negative impact of toxic leadership on the organization varies much between sectors of our society. Although we have focused on the military, those in other organizational contexts are likely to find much in these pages that is applicable. This is especially the case for contexts where a clear system of authority is in place, such as law enforcement, government, and highly regimented corporate structures. However, status, power, and hierarchy are present to some degree in all organizations, making the opportunities for abuse of authority ubiquitous. Some of the seemingly most structured and regimented military organizations actually operate in a surprisingly egalitarian fashion. Other organizations that appear to eschew titles, avoid obvious expressions of authority, and have relatively flat organizational charts actually have systems of status and power in place that rival the most hierarchical military units. Leadership is a process that can and does take place outside of authoritative positions, but power and leadership are closely, if not hopelessly, entwined.

Although we have not focused here on toxic subordinates or toxic colleagues, anyone who has served with them can attest to their negative impact. Toxic leaders, however, present the more intransigent problem because of the power differential that exists between military leaders and their subordinates. It is easier to deal with problematic colleagues and subordinates than with superiors who have the power to curtail careers and compel compliance with their orders. It can be difficult to watch out for a toxic peer, but bullying bosses are far harder to avoid, and the level of pain they can inflict is far greater. When a military organization selects an individual for a key leadership position, it sends a powerful message about the traits, personalities, characteristics, and behaviors it considers successful. In some respects by elevating such leaders the organization is validating them and setting them up as an example for others to emulate. For that reason alone it is important that the systems and processes that select and assign others to key leadership positions be attuned and sensitized to the identification and prevention of toxic leadership.

The U.S. military is entering a period of readjustment after over a decade of conflict that brought large appropriations. Many in the military today do not remember a time when parts and ammunition were in short supply, or when ships could not sail and planes could not fly due to insufficient funds in the training budget. The pay and benefits appropriated during wartime will come under increasing scrutiny as lawmakers seek to address the pressures associated with other budgetary priorities. A strong sense of mission that drives military personnel could wane. Just as combat brings leadership challenges, so too does peacetime. Good leadership will be essential in recruiting and retaining high quality military personnel as force reductions are put into effect. Appreciative and positive leadership styles that increase the level of fun, fellowship, and sense of meaning and purpose will be in demand.

Those who enter the U.S. military today are some of the most educated and motivated men and women to swear an oath to support and defend the Constitution. Their service is noble and should be celebrated. They deserve to be led in a way that honors their service and sacrifice. Poet William Ayot captured important sentiments about the two-way street of leadership in his poem "The Contract: A Word from the Led," which he has kindly allowed to be reprinted here as a fitting conclusion to this exploration of toxic leadership:

And in the end we follow them—
not because we are paid,
not because we might see some advantage,
not because of the things they have accomplished,
not even because of the dreams they dream,
but simply because of who they are;
the man, the woman, the leader, the boss,
standing up there when the wave hits the rock,
passing out faith and confidence like life jackets,
knowing the currents, holding the doubts,
imagining the delights and terrors of every landfall;
captain, pirate, and parent by turns,
the bearer of our countless hopes and expectations.
We give them our trust. We give them our effort.
What we ask in return is that they stay true.[15]

# NOTES

PREFACE

1. James MacGregor Burns, *Leadership* (New York: Harper & Row, 1978).
2. James MacGregor Burns, *The Lion and the Fox* (New York: Harcourt, Brace, 1956).
3. Joseph C. Rost, *Leadership for the Twenty-First Century*, foreword by James McGregor Burns (New York: Praeger, 1991), 102.

1. NATURE AND SCOPE OF TOXIC LEADERSHIP

1. Seth A. Rosenthal, *National Leadership Index 2012: A National Study of Confidence in Leadership* (Cambridge MA: Center for Public Leadership, Harvard Kennedy School, Harvard University, 2012), 4.
2. Rosenthal, *National Leadership Index 2012*.
3. James Fallows, "The Tragedy of the American Military," *Atlantic*, January–February 2015, http://www.theatlantic.com/features/archive/2014/12/the-tragedy-of-the-american-military/383516/.
4. Donald A. Davis, *Stonewall Jackson: Lessons in Leadership* (New York: Palgrave MacMillan, 2007), 32.
5. Paul Hersey, Kenneth H. Blanchard, and Dewey E. Johnson, *Management of Organizational Behavior*, 10th ed. (Upper Saddle River NJ: Prentice Hall, 2012).
6. Walter F. Ulmer Jr., "Toxic Leadership: What Are We Talking About?" *Army*, June 2012, 47–48.
7. R. Craig Bullis and George Reed, *Assessing Leaders to Establish and Maintain Positive Command Climate: A Report to the Secretary of the Army* (Carlisle Barracks PA: Army War College/Fairchild Research Information Center, 2003).

8. George E. Reed, "Toxic Leadership," *Military Review*, July–August 2004, 67–71.

9. James R. Meindl, Sanford B. Ehrlich, and Janet M. Dukerich, "The Romance of Leadership," *Administrative Science Quarterly* 30, no. 1 (1985): 78–102.

10. Barbara Kellerman, *Bad Leadership* (Boston MA: Harvard Business School Press, 2004), 11.

11. Roy F. Baumeister, Ellen Bratslavsky, Catrin Finkenauer, and Kathleen E. Vohs, "Bad Is Stronger Than Good," *Review of General Psychology* 5, no. 4 (2001): 323–70.

12. Denise F. Williams, *Toxic Leadership in the U.S. Army*, Strategy Research Project (Carlisle Barracks PA: Army War College, 2005), v–vi.

13. Jacobellis v. Ohio, 378 U.S. 184 (1964).

14. Jean Lipman-Blumen, *The Allure of Toxic Leaders: Why We Follow Destructive Bosses and Corrupt Politicians—And How We Can Survive Them* (New York: Oxford University Press, 2005), 17–18 (emphases in original).

15. Ståle Einarsen, Merethe Schanke Aasland, and Anders Skogstad, "Destructive Leadership Behaviour: A Definition and Conceptual Model," *Leadership Quarterly* 18, no. 3 (2007): 207–16.

16. Harvey A. Hornstein, *Brutal Bosses and Their Prey* (New York: Riverhead Books, 1996).

17. Hornstein, *Brutal Bosses*, 15–16.

18. Blake Ashforth, "Petty Tyranny in Organizations," *Human Relations* 47, no. 7 (1994): 755–78.

19. Ashforth, "Petty Tyranny."

20. Bennett J. Tepper, "Consequences of Abusive Supervision," *Academy of Management Journal* 43, no. 2 (2000): 178–90.

21. Department of the Army, *Army Leadership*, Army Doctrine Reference Publication (ADRP) No. 6-22. Washington DC: Headquarters, Department of the Army, 2012), http://armypubs.army.mil/doctrine/DR_pubs/dr_a/pdf/adrp6_22_new.pdf, 3.

22. Reed, "Toxic Leadership," 67. ADRP 6-22 describes the army view of leadership and was preceded by FM 22-100.

23. Marcia L. Whicker, *Toxic Leaders: When Organizations Go Bad* (Westport CT: Quorum Books, 1996), 61–63.

24. Whicker, *Toxic Leaders*, 118–20.

25. Paul Babiak and Robert D. Hare, *Snakes in Suits: When Psychopaths Go to Work* (New York: HarperCollins, 2006), 88.

26. Paul Babiak, Craig S. Neumann, and Robert D. Hare, "Corporate Psychopathy: Talking the Walk," *Behavioral Sciences and the Law* 28, no. 2 (2010): 174–93, p. 185.

27. Babiak et al., "Corporate Psychopathy," 192.

28. Babiak and Hare, *Snakes in Suits*.

29. Robert I. Sutton, *The No Asshole Rule: Building a Civilized Workplace and Surviving One That Isn't* (New York: Business Plus, 2007).

30. Sutton, *No Asshole Rule*, 2.

31. Sutton, *No Asshole Rule*, 9 (emphasis in original).

32. Sutton, *No Asshole Rule*.

33. Aristotle, "Ethica Eudemia," trans. J. Solomon, in *The Works of Aristotle*, vol. 9, ed. W. D. Ross (Oxford: Clarendon Press, 1925).

34. Tepper, "Consequences of Abusive Supervision," 262.

35. Michael Kusy and Elizabeth Holloway, *Toxic Workplace! Managing Toxic Personalities and Their Systems of Power* (San Francisco: Jossey-Bass, 2009), 5.

36. Brad C. Estes, "Abusive Supervision and Nursing Performance," *Nursing Forum* 48, no. 1 (2013): 3–16.

37. Christine Pearson and Christine Porath, *The Cost of Bad Behavior: How Incivility Is Damaging Your Business and What to Do about It* (New York: Portfolio, 2009).

38. Babiak et al., "Corporate Psychopathy," 183.

39. George E. Reed and R. Craig Bullis, "The Impact of Destructive Leadership on Senior Military Officers and Civilian Employees," *Armed Forces and Society* 36, no. 1 (2009): 5–18.

40. John Schaubroek, Fred O. Walumbwa, Daniel C. Ganster, and Sven Kepes, "Destructive Leader Traits and the Neutralizing Influence of an 'Enriched' Job," *Leadership Quarterly* 18, no. 3 (2007): 236–51.

41. George E. Reed and Richard A. Olsen, "Toxic Leadership: Part Deux," *Military Review* 90, no. 6 (2010): 58–64.

42. Jon J. Fallesen, "A Selective Review of Leadership Studies in the U.S. Army," *Military Psychology* 23, no. 5 (2011): 462–78.

43. Ryan Riley, Josh Hatfield, Art Paddock, and Jon J. Fallesen, *2012 Center for Army Leadership Annual Survey of Army Leadership (CASAL): Main Findings*, Technical Report 2013-1 (Fort Leavenworth KS: Center for Army Leadership, 2013).

44. Riley et al., *2012 CASAL*, 52.

## 2. IMPACT OF TOXIC LEADERSHIP

1. Thomas Carlyle, "On Heroes, Hero-Worship, and the Heroic in History," first published in vol. 1, *Carlyle's Complete Works*, 20 vol. Sterling ed. (Boston: Estes and Lauriat, n.d. [1884–]), available at http://www.gutenberg.org/files/1091/1091-h/1091-h.htm.

2. Joseph C. Rost, *Leadership for the Twenty-First Century* (Westport CT: Praeger, 1993).

3. George B. Graen and Mary Uhl-Bien, "Relationship-Based Approach to Leadership: Development of Leader-Member Exchange (LMX) Theory of Leadership over 25 Years: Applying a Multi-Level Multi-Domain Perspective," *Leadership Quarterly* 6, no. 2 (1995): 219–47.

4. Kathie L. Pelletier, "The Effects of Favored Status and Identification with the Victim on Perceptions and Reactions to Leader Toxicity" (PhD diss., Claremont Graduate University, 2009).

5. Pelletier, "Effects of Favored Status."

6. George E. Reed and R. Craig Bullis, "The Impact of Destructive Leadership on Senior Military Officers and Civilian Employees," *Armed Forces and Society* 36, no. 5 (2009): 5–18.

7. Abraham H. Maslow, "A Theory of Human Motivation," *Psychological Review* 50, no. 4 (1943): 370–96.

8. *Army Times* Staff, "In 2015 Army Will Lose Nearly 20,000 Soldiers in Drawdown," *Army Times*, December 27, 2014, http://www.armytimes.com/story/military/careers/army/2014/12/26/2015-drawdown-year-ahead/20860491/.

9. Andrew Tilghman, "DoD Braces for Political Battle over Military Pay," *Army Times*, December 30, 2014, http://www.armytimes.com/story/military/benefits/pay/2014/12/30/dod-prepares-for-compensation-report/21008055/.

10. Ted Koppel and Jack Smith, "The Deep Dive: One Company's Secret Weapon for Innovation," ABC News *Nightline*, original broadcast February 9, 1999 (New York: Films for the Humanities & Sciences/Films Media Group, 2006).

11. Hope H. Seck, "Chapter 1: A Worsening Morale Crisis," in "America's Military: A Force Adrift," *Military Times*, December 14, 2014, http://www.militarytimes.com/longform/military/2014/12/07/americas-military-a-force-adrift/18596571/.

12. Department of the Army, "Specialist Ross A. McGinnis, Medal of Honor, Operation Iraqi Freedom," Army.MIL Features, last updated June 12, 2013, http://www.army.mil/medalofhonor/mcginnis/.

13. Tim Duffy, *Military Experience and CEOs: Is There a Link?* (Los Angeles CA: Korn/Ferry International, 2006), http://www.kornferryinstitute.com/reports-insights/military-experience-and-ceos-there-link.

14. Inspector General of the Air Force, "Report of Investigation (S7033P): Maj Gen Stephen D. Schmidt," March 2013, http://s3.documentcloud.org/documents/1009999/redacted-schmidt-roi-for-foia-whitlock.pdf.

15. Inspector General, "Schmidt."

16. Inspector General, "Schmidt," 16.

17. Harvey A. Hornstein, *Brutal Bosses and Their Prey* (New York: Riverhead Books, 1996), 6.

18. Bennett J. Tepper, "Abusive Supervision in Work Organizations: Review Synthesis, and Research Agenda," *Journal of Management* 33, no. 3 (2007): 261–89.

19. Christine Porath and Christine Pearson, "The Price of Incivility," *Harvard Business Review*, January 2013, https://hbr.org/2013/01/the-price-of-incivility/.

20. Anthony T. Kern, "Darker Shades of Blue: A Case Study of Failed Leadership," Neil Krey's CRM Developers Forum [1995], https://web.archive.org/web/20140710182413/http://www.crm-devel.org/resources/paper/darkblue/darkblue.htm.

21. Bennett J. Tepper, "Consequences of Abusive Supervision," *Academy of Management Journal* 43, no. 2 (2000): 178–90.

22. Birgit Schyns and Jan Schilling, "How Bad Are the Effects of Bad Leaders? A Meta-Analysis of Destructive Leadership and Its Outcomes," *Leadership Quarterly* 24, no. 1 (2013): 138–58.

23. Mark Thompson, "The Rise and Fall of a Female Captain Bligh," *Time*, March 3, 2010, http://content.time.com/time/nation/article/0,8599,1969602,00.html.

24. Thompson, "Rise and Fall."

25. Peter A. Bamberger and Samuel B. Bacharach, "Abusive Supervision and Subordinate Problem Drinking: Taking Resistance, Stress, and Subordinate Personality into Account," *Human Relations* 59, no. 6 (2006): 723–52.

26. Ryan Riley, Josh Hatfield, Art Paddock, and Jon J. Fallesen, "2012 Center for Army Leadership Annual Survey of Army Leadership (CASAL): Main Findings," Technical Report 2013-1 (Fort Leavenworth KS: ICF International/Center for Army Leadership, 2013), http://usacac.army.mil/cac2/CAL/repository/2012CASALMainFindingsTechnicalReport2013-1.pdf.

27. Riley, "2012 Center," 16.
28. Riley, "2012 Center," 41–42.
29. Riley, "2012 Center," 51.
30. Kelly L. Zellars, Bennett J. Tepper, and Michelle K. Duffy, "Abusive Supervision and Subordinates' Organizational Citizenship Behavior," *Journal of Applied Psychology* 87, no. 6 (2002): 1068–76.
31. Reed and Bullis, "Impact of Destructive Leadership."
32. Reed and Bullis, "Impact of Destructive Leadership," 12.
33. James M. Dobbs, "The Relationship between Perceived Toxic Leadership Styles, Leader Effectiveness, and Organizational Cynicism" (PhD diss., University of San Diego, 2014).
34. Sean T. Hannah, John M. Schaubroeck, Ann C. Peng, Robert G. Lord, Linda K. Trevino, Steve W. J. Kozlowski, Bruce J. Avolio, Nikolaos Dimotakis, and Joseph Doty, "Joint Influences of Individual and Work Unit Abusive Supervision on Ethical Intentions and Behaviors: A Moderated Mediation Model," *Journal of Applied Psychology* 98, no. 4 (2013): 579–92.
35. Daniel Zwerdling, "Army Takes On Its Own Toxic Leaders," National Public Radio, *All Things Considered*, January 6, 2014, http://www.npr.org/2014/01/06/259422776/army-takes-on-its-own-toxic-leaders.
36. Zwerdling, "Army Takes On Its Own."
37. Philip Zimbardo, *The Lucifer Effect: Understanding How Good People Turn Evil* (New York: Random House, 2007).
38. Office of the Inspector General, Department of the Army, "(SES) Ms. Joyce Morrow, ROI 12-006 (Investigation Report for Preliminary Analysis DIG 12-0009)," Report of Investigation, February 4, 2013, http://s3.documentcloud.org/documents/1010000/morrow-ig-army.pdf.
39. Office of the Inspector General, "Ms. Joyce Morrow," 7.
40. Office of the Inspector General, "Ms. Joyce Morrow," 15.
41. Zwerdling, "Army Takes On Its Own."

3. CREATING AND SUSTAINING TOXIC LEADERS

1. Paul W. Mulvaney and Art Padilla, "The Environment of Destructive Leadership," in *When Leadership Goes Wrong*, ed. Brigit Schyns and Tiffany Hansbrough, 49–71 (Charlotte NC: Information Age, 2010), 50.
2. Mulvaney and Padilla, "Environment," 52–53.
3. Michael E. Kusy and Elizabeth L. Holloway, *Toxic Workplace! Managing Toxic Personalities and Their Systems of Power* (San Francisco: Jossey-Bass, 2009), 10.
4. Kusy and Holloway, *Toxic Workplace.*

5. Kusy and Holloway, *Toxic Workplace*, 71.
6. Daniel R. Denison, "What Is the Difference between Organizational Culture and Organizational Climate? A Native's Point of View on a Decade of Paradigm Wars," *Academy of Management Review* 21, no. 3 (1996): 619–54.
7. Edgar H. Schein, *Organizational Culture and Leadership*, 4th ed. (San Francisco: Jossey-Bass, 2010), 18.
8. Joanne Martin, *Organizational Culture: Mapping the Terrain* (Boston: Wadsworth, 2002), 361.
9. Diana McLain Smith, "Changing Culture Change," *Reflections* 12, no. 1 (2012): 1–13.
10. Anna Simons, "How Ambiguity Results in Excellence: The Role of Hierarchy and Reputation in U.S. Army Special Forces," *Human Organization* 57, no. 1 (1998): 117–23.
11. Simons, "How Ambiguity Results," 120–21.
12. Simons, "How Ambiguity Results," 121.
13. Schein, *Organizational Culture*, 300–313.
14. Lloyd J. Matthews, "The Uniformed Intellectual and His Place in American Arms, Part II: The Effects of Anti-Intellectualism on the Army Profession Today," *Army* 52, no. 8 (2002): 31–40, p. 32.
15. Steven Strasser, ed., *The Abu Ghraib Investigations* (New York: Public Affairs, 2004).
16. Guy B. Adams, Danny L. Balfour, and George E. Reed, "Abu Ghraib, Administrative Evil, and Moral Inversion: The Value of 'Putting Cruelty First,'" *Public Administration Review* 66, no. 5 (2006): 680–93.
17. Greg Botelho, "9 Air Force Commanders Fired from Jobs over Nuclear Missile Test Cheating," CNN.com, March 27, 2014, http://www.cnn.com/2014/03/27/us/air-force-cheating-investigation/.
18. Botelho, "9 Air Force Commanders."
19. Brian Everstine, "Nearly Half of Missileers at Malmstrom AFB Now Tied to Cheating Investigation," *Defense News*, January 30, 2014, http://www.defensenews.com/article/20140130/defreg02/301300038/Nearly-Half-Missileers-Malmstrom-AFB-Now-Tied-Cheating-Investigation.
20. Kusy and Holloway, *Toxic Workplace*, 30.
21. Mulvaney and Padilla, "Environment," 52.
22. Jean Lipman-Blumen, *The Allure of Toxic Leaders: Why We Follow Destructive Bosses and Corrupt Politicians—And How We Can Survive Them* (New York: Oxford University Press, 2005).
23. Lipman-Blumen, *Allure of Toxic Leaders*, 4.

24. Lipman-Blumen, *Allure of Toxic Leaders*, 31.
25. Lipman-Blumen, *Allure of Toxic Leaders*, 43.
26. Phillip G. Clampitt and Robert J. DeKoch, *Embracing Uncertainty: The Essence of Leadership* (Armonk NY: M. E. Sharpe, 2001).
27. Clampitt and DeKoch, *Embracing Uncertainty*.
28. Jean Lipman-Blumen, "Toxic Leadership: When Grand Illusions Masquerade as Noble Visions," *Leader to Leader*, Spring 2005, no. 36, 29–36.
29. Adams et al., "Abu Ghraib," 680–93.
30. Lipman-Blumen, "Toxic Leadership," 33.
31. Jay A. Conger, "The Dark Side of Leadership," *Organizational Dynamics* 19, no. 2 (1990): 44–55.
32. Conger, "Dark Side of Leadership," 55.
33. Ira Chaleff, *The Courageous Follower: Standing Up To and For Our Leaders* (San Francisco: Barrett-Koehler, 1995), 44.
34. Kusy and Holloway, *Toxic Workplace*, 30.
35. Pauline Rose Clance, *The Impostor Phenomenon: Overcoming the Fear That Haunts Your Success* (Atlanta: Peachtree, 1985).
36. Rory O'Brien McElwee and Tricia J. Yurak, "The Phenomenology of the Impostor Phenomenon," *Individual Differences Research* 8, no. 3 (2010): 184–97.
37. *There Will be Blood*, dir. Paul Thomas Anderson (2007; Hollywood CA: Paramount Home Entertainment, 2008).
38. John Stuart Mill, *Inaugural Address, Delivered to the University of St. Andrews, Feb. 1st 1867* (London: Longmans, Green, Reader, and Dyer), https://openlibrary.org/books/OL7089662M/Inaugural_address, 36.

4. THE ROLE OF NARCISSISM IN TOXIC LEADERSHIP

1. Seth A. Rosenthal and Todd L. Pittinsky, "Narcissistic Leadership," *Leadership Quarterly* 17, no. 6 (2006): 617–33.
2. Jean M. Twenge, Sara Konrath, Joshua D. Foster, W. Keith Campbell, and Brad J. Bushman, "Egos Inflating over Time: A Cross-Temporal Meta-Analysis of the Narcissistic Personality Inventory," *Journal of Personality* 76, no. 4 (2008): 875–902, p. 875.
3. Ronald E. Riggio, "Unholy Trio: Bullying, Cronism, and Narcissism. How and Why Workplace Bullies Thrive," *Psychology Today*, October 23, 2010, http://www.psychologytoday.com/blog/cutting-edge-leadership/201010/unholy-trio-bullying-cronyism-and-narcissism.
4. Riggio, "Unholy Trio."

5. *Enron: The Smartest Guys in the Room*, dir. Alex Gibney (2004; Los Angeles: Magnolia Home Entertainment, 2005).

6. Anton Myrer, *Once an Eagle* (New York: Holt, Rinehart and Winston, 1968).

7. Ronald E. Riggio, "What Is Grandiose Narcissism? Why Does It Matter?" *Psychology Today*, October 23, 2013, https://www.psychologytoday.com /blog/cutting-edge-leadership/201310/what-is-grandiose-narcissism-why -does-it-matter?collection=152711.

8. American Psychiatric Association, *Diagnostic and Statistical Manual of Mental Disorders*, 5th ed. (Arlington VA: American Psychiatric Publishing, 2013).

9. Michael Maccoby, "Narcissistic Leaders: The Incredible Pros, the Inevitable Cons," *Harvard Business Review* 82, no. 1 (2000): 92–101.

10. Maccoby, "Narcissistic Leaders," 96–98.

11. James Surowiecki, *The Wisdom of Crowds: Why the Many Are Smarter Than the Few and How Collective Wisdom Shapes Business, Economies, Societies and Nations* (New York: Anchor, 2005).

12. Sidney Walter Finkelstein, *Why Smart Executives Fail: And What You Can Learn from Their Mistakes* (New York: Portfolio, 2003), 214–38.

13. Peter Panzeri, *Little Big Horn 1876: Custer's Last Stand* (New York: Osprey, 1995), 17.

14. Richard Allan Fox Jr., *Archaeology, History, and Custer's Last Battle* (Norman: University of Oklahoma Press, 1993).

15. Ellen Nakashima, "Army Chief Uses Military Aircraft for House Deal," *Washington Post*, March 24, 2002, http://community.seattletimes .nwsource.com/archive/?date=20020324&slug=white24.

16. Eric Lichtblau, "Marines' Chief Investigator Visits El Toro in Flight Probe," *Los Angeles Times*, April 24, 1991, http://articles.latimes.com /1991-04-24/local/me-694_1_el-toro; Eric Lichtblau, "General's Appeal on Misuse of Aircraft Is Denied: Military: The Ex-Commander of Marine Western Air Bases Will Have a Letter of Reprimand Placed in His Permanent Record," *Los Angeles Times*, October 8, 1991, http:// articles.latimes.com/1991-10-08/local/me-238_1_u-s-marine-corps.

17. Finkelstein, *Why Smart Executives Fail*, 34–35.

18. Finkelstein, *Why Smart Executives Fail*, 231.

19. Rick Atkinson, *The Day of Battle: The War in Sicily and Italy, 1943–1945* (New York: Henry Holt, 2007), 33–34.

20. Riggio, "What Is Grandiose Narcissism?"

21. Joe Doty and Jeff Fenlason, "Narcissism and Toxic Leaders," *Military Review*, January–February 2013, 55–60.

22. John D. Mayer, Peter Salovey, and David R. Caruso, "Emotional Intelligence: Theory, Findings and Implications," *Psychological Inquiry* 15, no. 3 (2004): 197–215.

23. Daniel Goleman, *Emotional Intelligence* (New York: Bantam, 1995).

24. Chip Conley, "The Top 10 Emotionally-Intelligent Fortune 500 CEOs," *Huffington Post*, August 2, 2011, http://www.huffingtonpost.com/chip -conley/the-top-10-emotionallyint_b_911576.html.

25. Mayer et al., "Emotional Intelligence," 209–10.

26. Nona Momeni, "The Relation between Managers' Emotional Intelligence and the Organizational Climate They Create," *Public Personnel Management* 38, no. 2 (2009): 35–48.

27. Department of Defense, "Instruction Number 6490.04, Mental Health Evaluations of Members of the Military Services," March 4, 2013, http:// www.dtic.mil/whs/directives/corres/pdf/649004p.pdf.

28. Maccoby, "Narcissistic Leaders," 99.

5. TOXIC LEADERSHIP AND SEXUAL MISCONDUCT

1. Edwin P. Hollander, "Conformity, Status, and Idiosyncrasy Credit," *Psychological Review* 65, no. 2 (1958): 117–27.

2. N. N. Sarker and Rina Sarker, "Sexual Assault on Woman: Its Impact on Her Life and Living in Society," *Sexual Relationship Therapy* 20, no. 4 (2005): 407–19.

3. Margaret E. Bell, Jessica A. Turchik, and Julie A. Karpenko, "Impact of Gender on Reactions to Military Sexual Assault and Harassment," *Health and Social Work* 39, no. 1 (2014): 25–33.

4. Dan Lamothe, "Here's How Disgraced Brig. Gen. Jeffrey Sinclair's Affair Will Hit Him in the Wallet," *Washington Post*, June 20, 2014, http:// www.washingtonpost.com/news/checkpoint/wp/2014/06/20/heres-how -disgraced-brig-gen-jeffrey-sinclair-got-demoted-two-ranks/.

5. Craig Whitlock, "Military Brass, Behaving Badly: Files Detail a Spate of Misconduct Dogging Armed Forces," *Washington Post*, January 26, 2014, http://www.washingtonpost.com/world/national-security/military -brass-behaving-badly-files-detail-a-spate-of-misconduct-dogging-armed -forces/2014/01/26/4d06c770-843d-11e3-bbe5-6a2a3141e3a9_story.html.

6. Michael D. Shear, "Petraeus Quits: Evidence of Affair Was Found by FBI," *New York Times*, November 9, 2012, http://www.nytimes.com/2012 /11/10/us/citing-affair-petraeus-resigns-as-cia-director.html.

7. Department of Defense, Sexual Assault Prevention and Response, *Department of Defense Annual Report on Sexual Assault in the Military, Fiscal Year 2013*, vol. 1 (Washington DC: Department of Defense, 2014), http://www.sapr.mil/public/docs/reports/FY13_DoD_SAPRO_Annual_Report_on_Sexual_Assault.pdf.

8. Melissa S. Herbert, *Camouflage Isn't Only for Combat: Gender, Sexuality and Women in the Military* (New York: New York University Press, 1998).

9. L. Michael Allsep Jr. "The Myth of the Warrior: Masculinity and the End of Don't Ask, Don't Tell," *Journal of Homosexuality* 60 (2013): 281–400.

10. Department of Defense, Sexual Assault Prevention and Response, *Annual Report on Sexual Harassment and Violence at the Military Service Academies, Academic Program Year 2012–2013* (Washington DC: Department of Defense, 2013), http://www.sapr.mil/public/docs/reports/FINAL_APY_12-13_MSA_Report.pdf.

11. Christopher P. Krebs, Christine H. Lindquist, Tara D. Warner, Bonnie S. Fisher, and Sandra L. Martin, *The Campus Sexual Assault (CSA) Study: Final Report* (Washington DC: National Institute of Justice for the U.S. Department of Justice, 2007), https://www.ncjrs.gov/pdffiles1/nij/grants/221153.pdf.

12. Department of Defense, *Sexual Harassment and Violence*, 5.

13. Department of Defense, *Sexual Assault in the Military*.

14. Bridgit Burns, Kate Grindlay, Kelsey Holt, Ruth Manski, and Daniel Grossman, "Military Sexual Trauma among US Servicewomen during Deployment: A Qualitative Study," *American Journal of Public Health* 104, no. 2 (2014): 345–49.

15. Burns et al., "Military Sexual Trauma," 347.

16. Department of Defense, *Evaluation of the Military Criminal Investigative Organizations Sexual Assault Investigations*, Report DODIG-2013-091, July 9, 2013, Alexandria VA: Department of Defense, Inspector General, 2013), http://www.dodig.mil/pubs/documents/DODIG-2013-091.pdf.

17. Department of Defense, *Sexual Assault Investigations*, 7.

18. Department of Defense, *Sexual Assault Investigations*, 68.

19. Department of Defense, *Sexual Assault Investigations*, 68

20. Testimony of Rebekah Havrilla, Senate Armed Services Committee, Sub-Committee on Personnel, Hearing on Military Sexual Violence, 103rd Congress, 1st sess., March 13, 2013.

21. James Dao, "In Debate over Sexual Assault, Men Are Overlooked Victims," *New York Times*, June 23, 2013, http://www.nytimes.com/2013/06/24/us/in-debate-over-military-sexual-assault-men-are-overlooked-victims.html.

22. Testimony of Brian K. Lewis, Senate Armed Services Committee, Sub-Committee on Personnel, Hearing on Military Sexual Violence, 103rd Congress, 1st sess., March 13, 2013.

23. Testimony of Brian K. Lewis.

24. Terry L. Price, *Understanding Ethical Failures in Leadership* (New York: Cambridge University Press, 2006).

25. Price, *Understanding Ethical Failures*, 50.

26. Dean C. Ludwig and Clinton O. Longenecker, "The Bathsheba Syndrome: The Ethical Failure of Successful Leaders," *Journal of Business Ethics* 12, no. 4 (1993): 265–73.

27. Ludwig and Longenecker, "Bathsheba Syndrome," 271.

28. Ludwig and Longenecker, "Bathsheba Syndrome," 271–72.

29. Ronald A. Heifetz and Martin Linsky, *Leadership on the Line: Staying Alive through the Dangers of Leading* (Boston: Harvard Business Press, 2002), 164.

30. Linsky and Heifetz, *Leadership on the Line*, 177.

31. Linsky and Heifetz, *Leadership on the Line*, 182.

32. United States Military Academy, *Building Capacity to Lead: The West Point System for Leader Development* (West Point NY: United States Military Academy, 2009), vi.

33. Dean Calbreath, "Anatomy of a Bribe: Ex-Lawmaker's Web of Cash, Contracts," *Union Tribune San Diego*, March 4, 2006, http://legacy.utsandiego.com/news/politics/cunningham/20060304-9999-1n4anatomy.html.

### 6. SURVIVING A TOXIC LEADER

1. Jean Lipman-Blumen, *The Allure of Toxic Leaders: Why We Follow Destructive Bosses and Corrupt Politicians—And How We Can Survive Them* (New York: Oxford University Press, 2005).

2. Uniform Code of Military Justice, U.S. Code, Title 10, Chapter 47.

3. Robert Sutton, "Tips for Surviving Workplace Assholes: If You Can't Escape Right Now," *Bloomberg Businessweek*, July 2, 2009, http://www.businessweek.com/business_at_work/bad_bosses/archives/2008/07/bad_boss.html.

4. Linnda Durré, *Surviving the Toxic Workplace: Protect Yourself against the Co-workers, Bosses, and Work Environments That Poison Your Day* (New York: McGraw-Hill, 2010).

5. Marcia L. Whicker, *Toxic Leaders: When Organizations Go Bad* (Westport CT: Quorum Books, 1996), 177.

6. Sutton, "Tips for Surviving."

7. Whicker, *Toxic Leaders*, 177.

8. Harvey A. Hornstein, *Brutal Bosses and Their Prey* (New York: Riverhead Books, 1996), 145.

9. Hornstein, *Brutal Bosses*.

10. Tom Roeder, "'Toxic' Fort Carson Battalion Commander Returns to Job Despite Recommendation of Firing," *The Gazette* [Colorado Springs CO], October 22, 2014, http://gazette.com/toxic-fort-carson-battalion -commander-returns-to-job-despite-recommendation-of-firing/article /1539975.

11. Roeder, "Fort Carson Battalion Commander."

12. Roeder, "Fort Carson Battalion Commander."

13. Marshall Goldsmith and Mark Reiter, *What Got You Here Won't Get You There* (New York: Hyperion, 2007).

14. Goldsmith and Reiter, *What Got You Here*, 7.

15. Goldsmith and Reiter, *What Got You Here*.

16. Scott Fontaine, "IG: 2-Star Passed Over Whistle-Blower Colonel," *Air Force Times*, June 12, 2011, http://www.airforcetimes.com/article/20110612 /NEWS/106120315/IG-2-star-passed-over-whistle-blower-colonel.

17. Fontaine, "2-Star Passed."

18. Sutton, "Tips for Surviving."

19. 10 U.S. Code § 938, Art. 138, Complaint of Wrongs.

20. Marco Tavanti, "Managing Toxic Leaders: Dysfunctional Patterns in Organizational Leadership and How to Deal with Them," *Human Resource Management*, no. 6 (2011): 127–36.

21. Michael E. Kusy and Elizabeth L. Holloway, *Toxic Workplace! Managing Toxic Personalities and Their Systems of Power* (San Francisco: Jossey-Bass, 2009).

22. Colin Powell and Joseph E. Persico, *My American Journey* (New York, Ballentine Books, 1995), 50.

23. Judith W. Umlas, *Grateful Leadership: Using the Power of Acknowledgment to Engage All Your People and Achieve Superior Results* (New York, McGraw-Hill, 2013).

24. Aaron B. Wildavsky, *Speaking Truth to Power: The Art and Craft of Policy Analysis* (Boston: Little, Brown, 1979).

25. George S. Patton Jr., "General George S. Patton, Jr. Quotations," The Official Website of General George S. Patton, Jr., n.d., http://www .generalpatton.com/quotes/.

26. James C. Collins, *How the Mighty Fall: And Why Some Companies Never Give In* (New York: HarperCollins, 2009), 81.

27. Robert Earl Kelley, *The Power of Followership: How to Create Leaders People Want to Follow, and Followers Who Lead Themselves* (New York: Doubleday, 1992).

28. Ira Chaleff, *The Courageous Follower: Standing Up To and For Our Leaders* (San Francisco: Berrett-Koehler, 1998).

29. Chaleff, *Courageous Follower.*

30. Julie Irwin, "Loyalty to a Leader Is Overrated, Even Dangerous," *Harvard Business Review,* December 16, 2004, https://hbr.org/2014/12 /loyalty-to-a-leader-is-overrated-even-dangerous/.

31. Irwin, "Loyalty to a Leader."

32. Mark E. Cantrell, "The Doctrine of Dissent," *Marine Corps Gazette* 82, no. 11 (1998): 56–57.

33. Debra E. Meyerson, *Rocking the Boat: How to Effect Change without Making Trouble* (Boston: Harvard Business Press, 2008).

7. TOXIC COWORKERS

1. Gary Namie, *2014 WBI U.S. Workplace Bullying Survey* (Bellingham WA: Workplace Bullying Institute, 2014), 10, http://workplacebullying. org/multi/pdf/WBI-2014-US-Survey.pdf.

2. Alan A. Cavaiola and Neil J. Lavender, *Toxic Coworkers: How to Deal with Dysfunctional People on the Job* (Oakland CA: New Harbinger, 2000), 4–5.

3. Namie, *Workplace Bullying Survey,* 12.

4. Joint Commission on Accreditation of Healthcare Organizations, *Defusing Disruptive Behavior: A Workbook for Health Care Leaders* (Oakbrook Terrace IL: Joint Commission Resources, 2007).

5. College of Licensed Practical Nurses of Alberta, *Practice Guideline: Addressing Co-worker Abuse in the Workplace* (Edmonton: College of Licensed Practical Nurses of Alberta, 2013), http://www.clpna.com/wp -content/uploads/2013/02/doc_Practice_Guideline_Addressing_Co -Worker_Abuse_Workplace.pdf.

6. Robert M. Bramson, *Coping with Difficult People* (New York: Dell, 1981).

7. Bramson, *Coping with Difficult People,* 187.

8. Paul Babiak and Robert D. Hare, *Snakes in Suits: When Psychopaths Go to Work* (New York: HarperCollins, 2006).

9. Babiak and Hare, *Snakes in Suits,* 312.

10. Donald G. Dutton and Susan Painter, "Emotional Attachments in Abusive Relationships: A Test of Traumatic Bonding Theory," *Violence and Victims* 8, no. 2 (1993): 105–20.

11. Christopher Klein, "The Birth of 'Stockholm Syndrome,' 40 Years Ago," History.com, August 23, 2013, http://www.history.com/news/stock holm-syndrome.

12. Chris Cantor and John Price, "Traumatic Entrapment, Appeasement and Complex Post-Traumatic Stress Disorder: Evolutionary Perspectives of Hostage Reactions, Domestic Abuse and the Stockholm Syndrome," *Australian and New Zealand Journal of Psychiatry* 41, no. 5 (2007): 377–84.

13. Richard S. Lazarus and Susan Folkman, *Stress, Appraisal, and Coping* (New York: Springer, 1984).

14. Workplace Bullying Institute, "Stress-Related Health Impairment: How Bullying Can Affect Your Brain and Body," Workplace Bullying Institute, [2012], http://www.workplacebullying.org/individuals/impact /physical-health-harm/.

15. Craig E. Johnson, *Meeting the Ethical Challenges of Leadership: Casting Light or Shadow*, 3rd ed. (Los Angeles: Sage, 2009), 111.

16. Johnson, *Meeting the Ethical Challenges*, 116.

17. Laura Hillenbrand, *Unbroken: A World War II Story of Survival, Resilience, and Redemption* (New York: Random House, 2010); *Unbroken*, dir. Angelina Jolie (2014; Los Angeles: Universal Pictures, 2015).

18. Louis Zamperini and David Rensin, *Devil at My Heels: A Heroic Olympian's Astonishing Story of Survival as a Japanese POW in World War II* (New York: HarperCollins, 2003).

19. E. D. and G. E. W. Scobie, "Damaging Events: The Perceived Need for Forgiveness," *Journal for the Theory of Social Behavior* 28, no. 4 (1998): 373–402, p. 397.

8. MITIGATING TOXIC LEADERSHIP

1. Harvey A. Hornstein, *Brutal Bosses and Their Prey* (New York: Riverhead Books, 1996).

2. Alan Goldman, "Company on the Couch: Unveiling Toxic Behavior in Dysfunctional Organizations," *Journal of Management Inquiry* 17, no. 3 (2008): 226–38.

3. Irving L. Janis, "Groupthink: The Desperate Drive for Consensus at Any Cost," *Psychology Today* 5 (1971): 43–76.

4. Michael E. Kusy and Elizabeth L. Holloway, *Toxic Workplace! Managing Toxic Personalities and Their Systems of Power* (San Francisco: Jossey-Bass, 2009).

5. Paul C. Nystrom and William H. Starbuck, "To Avoid Organizational Crises, Unlearn," *Organizational Dynamics* 12, no. 4 (1984): 53–65.

6. Daniel Goleman, *Emotional Intelligence* (New York: Bantam, 1995).

7. Goleman, *Emotional Intelligence*, 58.

8. Goldman, "Company on the Couch," 237.

9. Colin Powell and Joseph E. Persico, *My American Journey* (New York: Ballantine, 1995), 52.

10. George E. Reed and Craig R. Bullis, "The Impact of Destructive Leadership on Senior Military Officers and Civilian Employees," *Armed Forces and Society* 36, no. 1 (2009): 5–18, p. 13.

11. Thom Shanker, "Conduct at Issue as Military Officers Face a New Review," *New York Times*, April 13, 2013, http://www.nytimes.com/2013/04/14/us/militarys-top-officers-face-review-of-their-character.html.

12. Bullis and Reed, "Impact of Destructive Leadership," 13.

13. Walter F. Ulmer Jr., "Toxic Leadership: What Are We Talking About?" *Army Magazine*, June 2012, 47–48, p. 52.

14. Robert I. Sutton, *The No Asshole Rule: Building a Civilized Workplace and Surviving One That Isn't* (New York: Business Plus, 2007).

15. Thomas E. Ricks, *The Generals: American Military Command from World War II to Today* (New York: Penguin, 2012).

16. Gregg F. Martin, George E. Reed, Ruth B. Collins, and Cortez K. Dial, "The Road to Mentoring: Paved with Good Intentions," *Parameters* 32, no. 3 (2002): 115–27.

17. Peter J. Varljen, *Leadership: More Than Mission Accomplishment* (Carlisle Barracks PA: USAWC Strategy Research Project, 2001).

18. Dirk Lindebaum, "Rhetoric or Remedy? A Critique on Developing Emotional Intelligence," *Academy of Management Learning and Education* 8, no. 2 (2009): 225–37.

19. Sean D. Naylor, "Keane Blames Leadership for Junior Officer Exodus," *Army Times*, 25 December 2000, 10.

20. Naylor, "Keane Blames Leadership," 50.

CONCLUSION

1. Orson Scott Card, *Ender's Game* (New York: Tom Doherty Associates, 1977).

2. *Ender's Game*, dir. Gavin Hood (2013; Santa Monica CA: Summit Entertainment, 2014).

3. Daniel Zwerdling, Army Takes On Its Own Toxic Leaders," National Public Radio, *All Things Considered*, January 6, 2014, http://www.npr .org/2014/01/06/259422776/army-takes-on-its-own-toxic-leaders.
4. Dianna Cahn, "USS James E. Williams' Toxic Command Climate Cited in Sailor's Suicide," *Stars and Stripes*, December 17, 2014, http://www .stripes.com/news/navy/uss-james-e-williams-toxic-command-climate -cited-in-sailor-s-suicide-1.319730.
5. Cahn, "USS James E. Williams."
6. Cahn, "USS James E. Williams."
7. Immanuel Kant, *Grounding for the Metaphysics of Morals*, 3rd ed., trans. James W. Ellington (1785; Indianapolis: Hackett, 1993).
8. Craig Whitlock, "Toxic on Top," *Stars and Stripes*, February 1, 2014, http://estripes.osd.mil/download/MID_MID_010214.pdf; Zwerdling, "Army Takes On Its Own."
9. Jacquelyn Scarville, Scott B. Button, Jack E. Edwards, Anita R. Lancaster, and Timothy W. Elig, "Armed Forces Equal Opportunity Survey," DMDC Report No. 97-027. (Arlington VA: Defense Manpower Data Center, 1999), http://www.dtic.mil/dtic/tr/fulltext/u2/a366037 .pdf.
10. Robert J. House, "A Path Goal Theory of Leader Effectiveness," *Administrative Science Quarterly* 16, no. 3 (1971): 321–39.
11. Ronald E. Riggio, "4 Ways Your Boss Could Ruin Your Work Career," *Psychology Today*, December 19, 2014, http://www.psychologytoday .com/blog/cutting-edge-leadership/201412/4-ways-your-boss-could-ruin -your-work-career.
12. Michael E. Kusy and Elizabeth L. Holloway, *Toxic Workplace! Managing Toxic Personalities and Their Systems of Power* (San Francisco: Jossey-Bass, 2009).
13. Don Snider and Lloyd Matthews, eds., *The Future of the Army Profession*, 2nd ed. (Boston: McGraw-Hill, 2005).
14. James Q. Wilson, *Bureaucracy: What Government Agencies Do and Why They Do It* (New York: Basic Books, 1991).
15. William Ayot, *E-Mail from the Soul* (Glastonbury, United Kingdom: Avalon, 2012).

# INDEX

psychological type theory, 123
psychopathy and psychopaths, 18,
    23, 118, 139
public humiliation of
    subordinates, 124
public interest, personal interests
    as, 77–78, 101
public resources,
    misappropriation of, 77–78
purpose, pursuit of, 33

rape. *See* sexual assault
*Reader's Digest*, 32
recruitment, toxic leadership's
    impact on, 37
removal and reassignment, 119,
    122–23, 155–56, 169
reputation: and dealing with toxic
    coworkers, 137; social credit
    and, 87–88
resources, access to, 102
responsibility, in military culture,
    57
retention, toxic leadership's
    impact on, 37
Ricks, Thomas, 155–56
Riggio, Ronald E., 68–69, 166
risk, denial of, 129
romance of leadership, 9
Roosevelt, Theodore, 81
Root, Elihu, 80
Rost, Joseph, 28
Ruby, Tom, 5

Salovey, Peter, 82
Samsung Motors, 78
satisfaction, inverse relationship
    between destructive leadership
    and, 41
Schein, Edgar, 50, 52

Schofield, John M., 1
Schultz, Howard, 83
self-assessment, 126–27, 149–50
self-awareness, 38, 117–18, 167
self-interest, motivation by,
    15–16
self-promotion, 42
senior military personnel:
    behavior under toxic
    leadership, 41; influence of,
    151–52; and sexual misconduct,
    89–90, 96
sexual assault: congressional
    interventions and, 96–100;
    investigation of, 92–94, 97
sexual misconduct: character
    and, 105–7; congressional
    interventions and, 96–100;
    impact of, 88–90; and military
    culture, 90–95; reasons for,
    101–5
silver linings, 114–15
Simons, Anna, 51–52
situational leadership, 7
Skilling, Jeffrey, 69–70
Smith, Frederick W., 160
Snider, Don, 170
social credit and status, 87–88
social support system, 113
Spanish American War, 80–81
special forces teams, cultures of,
    51–52
spokespeople, narcissists as
    company, 79–80
Stanford prison experiment,
    44–45
Starbuck, William H., 145
Stewart, Potter, 11
Stockholm syndrome, 139–40
street fighters, 17